THE **5** CHOICES™
to extraordinary productivity

"Extraordinary productivity is not about time management, it's about managing your decisions, attention, and energy."
–Leigh Stevens

A BRIEF MONOGRAPH

Table of Contents

The 5 Choices to Extraordinary Productivity

"The crime which bankrupts men and nations is that of turning aside from one's main purpose to serve a job here and there."
—Ralph Waldo Emerson

You're already a productive person. You get up in the morning, you go to work, and you do the best you can to enjoy life and take care of your responsibilities to the people who depend on you.

But deep down, you feel that maybe there's more for you. You want to make more of a difference. You could probably do better, contribute more, get more out of life. Maybe you feel you're shortchanging yourself in some ways. But you do what you can, and frankly, you don't have the time or energy to do much more than you're already doing.

That's why the idea of improving your productivity might make you sigh a little. On one hand, you'd like to be more productive. But on the other hand, it sounds like more work—and you have enough of that to do now. People already expect more from you than you can give. They're always asking you to "do more with less," aren't they?

Yes, they are. But you both have a misguided idea of what productivity really is. It's not doing more. In fact, it means doing *less*.

Most of us try to do too much, and as a result, we give less than our best and finest effort to those few things that really matter. Extraordinarily productive people consciously choose to invest that effort only where they can *contribute most*.

They give their best to the people and things that excite them, that fill them with purpose, that really *count*.

It took Michelangelo four totally focused years to paint the ceiling of the Sistine Chapel. What if he had chosen to fragment his time among many less monumental projects?

What if William Shakespeare had been too busy with the theater business to write his plays?

What if Steve Jobs had made a thousand mediocre products instead of a handful of "insanely great" products?

What if Rosa Parks had decided she had too many things to do that day to risk going to jail by defying an unjust law?

What if Albert Einstein had been so stressed out at his patent-office job that he never took time to think about the universe?

And what if Martin Luther King, Jr. had never had a dream?

These and so many other people show us what it means to be *extraordinarily* productive. They transform the world in quantum ways. They have an exponential impact because they focus intensely on the unique contribution only *they* can make.

"But I'm no Einstein," you say. "I'm just an ordinary person—there's nothing extraordinary about me."

The truth is, we all have extraordinary things to do in our own Circle of Influence. It's tragic if, as Emerson said, we "turn aside from our main purpose to serve a job here and there."

How We Use Our Work Time

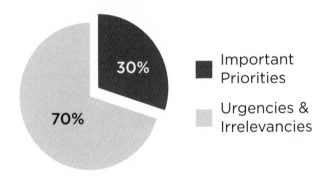

From the FranklinCovey Time Matrix Survey of 351,613 respondents (as of 2011) from Africa, Asia-Pacific, Europe, Latin America, Middle East, and North America, ongoing since 2005.[1]

- We typically spend about 70 percent of the workday on problems, crises, and and activities that do not contribute to the true priorities of the organization. Because we feel we have to "serve a job here and there," we shortchange our "main purpose."

- We never get clear on our "main purpose"—the extraordinary contribution we *could* make in the roles we play in work and life.

- We work and live by *default*—dealing with whatever comes up—instead of by *design*—focusing our finest and best effort on those things with the greatest payoff.

- We've been hijacked by our technology. Flooded with electronic distractions, we've allowed our productivity tools to make us unproductive!

- We burn out our brains and bodies because our lives are not our own—we have no time for building up our own productive capacity.

By contrast, extraordinarily productive people—

- Reclaim the 70 percent of the workday that is spent on lower-value activities.

- Know the extraordinary contribution they want to make at work and to the lives of the people who are important to them.

- Block out time specifically to make those contributions real.

- Leverage their technology. Instead of ninety emails a day, they have nine—but each one is strategically important.

- Refresh and recharge themselves regularly so they can continue to be productive.

These people get amazing results because they act differently, and they act differently because they *think* differently. The enemy of the extraordinary is not our capability—it's our mindset!

The Productivity Paradox

There is no time like the present. There never was.

At no other time in history have we been able to do the things we can do today—extraordinary things beyond the imagining of people just a few years ago.

Our information technology has greatly expanded our powers. We can access nearly all human knowledge in seconds. We can communicate with anyone anywhere. By touching a screen, we can buy a book and start reading it in the same moment. Our smartphones are far smarter than we are.

This should be the Age of Extraordinary Productivity.

But it isn't.

For years, economists have been puzzled by what they call the "productivity paradox." The vast investment by business and government in information technology has not significantly increased productivity, at least by the traditional measure of output per worker per hour. In fact, there has been a long, slow decline in productivity worldwide since 1971.

It's hard to believe. Hasn't the digital revolution exponentially improved productivity? Isn't it true that jobs that used to take all day and cost hundreds of dollars now take a nanosecond and cost a nano-cent? Yes. Digitization has transformed countless processes of all kinds. But it has not made human beings themselves more productive.

We don't have to look far to see why. The knowledge work of today is fundamentally different from the industrial work of the past. However, we have not yet escaped the mindset of the Industrial Age, even though we're well into the Knowledge Age.

Look at these radical differences between Industrial Age and Knowledge Age workers:

	Industrial Age	Knowledge Age
Choices	Few	Unlimited
Decisions	Simple, Low Value	Complex, High Value
Tools	Straightforward	Complicated and Disruptive

During the Industrial Age, workers on an assembly line put one part on one machine a hundred times a day. They had few choices and fewer decisions to make. Decisions they did have to make were simple and of low value. Their tools had one, straightforward use.

As knowledge workers, we no longer stand in an assembly line doing repetitive tasks. We have comparatively unlimited choices about what to work on, when, and how. ("Do I answer this email? accept this meeting invitation? work on this project or that one?")

And unless we are crystal clear on what we're trying to achieve, there are infinite ways to get "there"—wherever it is.

We're asked to make complex decisions, many of which can have high value to the organization. For example, a salesperson's decisions on how to use her time can translate into millions of dollars' difference to the bottom line.

Digital technology can make it both far easier and far harder to be extraordinarily productive. Our complex tools can do far more than we are prepared to do with them. Their potential for increasing our productivity is limitless—and so is their potential for disruption.

Overwhelming in its impact, the technology that's reshaping our lives is not only incredibly useful, but also alluring. For example, avid blogger Nicholas Carr confesses himself addicted to email, random links, Google, MP3s, streaming video, YouTube, and Wikipedia—all at the swipe of a finger on his iPad. Like millions of us, he has developed a hunger to be connected.

But now Carr is worried. "Over the last few years, I've had an uncomfortable sense that someone or something has been tinkering with my brain.... I'm not thinking the way I used to think.... I worry about my inability to pay attention to one thing for more than a couple of minutes."[2]

And that's because he has so much more to pay attention to. Everyone knows that the information explosion is huge, but it's almost incomprehensible how huge. By the end of the 20th century, the entire sum of information produced since the dawn of civilization was about 12 exabytes. We now produce this much information in about four days. Within the first decade of the 21st century, annual traffic on the Internet approached 1,000 exabytes, or 19 million times the volume of information contained in all the books ever written.[3] But that was just a trickle: the flood is about to surpass one zettabyte, or the equivalent of the contents of 50 million Libraries of Congress.[4] (The largest in the world, the Library of Congress in Washington, D.C., contains nearly 150 million items.)

And our personal information explosion is also huge.

In fact, we might be in serious danger of drowning under a tsunami of texts, tweets, IMs, emails, and infinite social-media updates. We used to get interrupted occasionally. Now the interruptions have become a torrent. Brain scientists are telling us that our 21st-century addiction to information may actually be rewiring our brains and shrinking to nearly zero our ability to concentrate.

The productivity paradox applies to people too. What's true for business in general is also true for each of us as individuals.

Our powerful knowledge tools now put truly extraordinary productivity within the reach of everyone.

EXTRAORDINARY PRODUCTIVITY

But the same tools that promise to make us exponentially more productive also create exponentially more distractions than we've ever had to face. We're at risk of being mastered by our own tools and buried alive in an avalanche of information.

BURIED ALIVE

To be specific:

- Ninety-four percent of knowledge workers at some point have felt overwhelmed by information to the point of incapacity.

- Knowledge workers say they waste 28 percent of their time on unimportant interruptions to the point that they can devote only about 5 percent of their time to thought and reflection.

- The average knowledge worker receives 93 emails a day. Spending five minutes on each message would eat up an entire workday.[5]

- Over 107 trillion emails are sent each year, of which 89 percent are spam.[6]

- About half (51 percent) of all professionals surveyed around the world say that if the amount of information they receive continues to increase, they will soon reach a "breaking point" at which they will be unable to handle any more.[7]

The problem is, each message represents a person who needs or wants something from you. You want to be accommodating, but when you're buried under a landslide of commitments, the whole idea of productive work evaporates.

The Choice: To Be Extraordinarily Productive or Buried Alive?

What can we do about this exhausting paradox we live with?

We can't ignore the reality that the human brain is a splendid tool for focusing on a few things at a time, but a poor tool for handling a lot of things at once. As the Roman philosopher Seneca said, "To be everywhere is to be nowhere."

One answer is to try to get everything done and out of the way—then (we tell ourselves) we'll be able to concentrate. We think if we can just sit down and make a giant to-do list, systematically work through it, and attend to everybody's priorities, we'll be able to focus. Many of us live with that fantasy. The problem is, while we're taking care of the things at the top of the list, the bottom of the list is growing out of control. It's like shoveling gravel from a pile that gets bigger the more we dig at it.

Another answer is to file everything—create folders for all the people and projects at work and dump everything in those folders. This has the advantage of moving everything off your desktop and out of sight. The problem with sweeping the gravel under the rug is that the rug starts to get lumpy and hard to walk on. All you've succeeded in doing is to sort the gravel into little piles. You haven't actually done anything useful with it. And while you're sorting and categorizing and filing the old gravel, the stream of new gravel never stops.

Ironically, we waste so much time and energy on the gravel that we're too tired and pressed for time to attend to the "Big Rocks"—those really important things we keep putting off.

This is the situation of people who "live out of their inbox." Many of us start work by checking email. It's essential. What do people want from us today? Also, it's irresistible. We crave new information and can't stand to miss anything. We start the day intending to get something important done, but then the inbox takes over, and before we know it, the day is gone.

And if we spend our best energy on the gravel of miscellaneous demands, what's left for the truly important priorities?

Brain science helps us understand why we don't multitask effectively. Although the creative potential of the mind is unlimited, the gateway to the mind is strictly limited. Only one or two things at a time can get in, so they'd better be the *most important things—the right things.*

The 5 Choices

Fortunately, there are 5 Choices that, if made consistently, can make you extraordinarily productive—not just by getting things done, but by getting the *right* things done. The 5 Choices help you distinguish between the vitally important things that can transform your life and work, and all the distractions and irrelevancies that threaten to bury you alive.

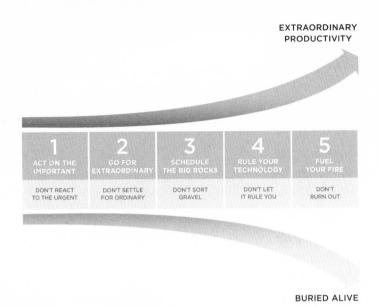

EXTRAORDINARY
PRODUCTIVITY

1	2	3	4	5
ACT ON THE IMPORTANT	GO FOR EXTRAORDINARY	SCHEDULE THE BIG ROCKS	RULE YOUR TECHNOLOGY	FUEL YOUR FIRE
DON'T REACT TO THE URGENT	DON'T SETTLE FOR ORDINARY	DON'T SORT GRAVEL	DON'T LET IT RULE YOU	DON'T BURN OUT

BURIED ALIVE

The 5 Choices. Making these choices can lead you to extraordinary levels of productivity. Defaulting on these choices can make you feel buried alive under the weight of conflicting demands.

Choice 1: Act on the Important, Don't React to the Urgent. Many people think if they could just do more things faster, they'd be more productive. Their brains are hijacked by incoming demands; they lose the ability to discern between important and unimportant priorities.

By contrast, extraordinarily productive people don't just react to the "incoming." They carefully discern important from unimportant priorities, and they are proactive about investing their time only in those things that deserve their finest effort and attention.

This is the first choice to make if you want an extraordinary life. Many people fail to realize they have the power to choose for themselves how they will live and work. They see themselves as victims of their circumstances. But if you make Choice 1, you literally take charge of your life. You're free to create your own future.

Choice 2: Go for Extraordinary, Don't Settle for Ordinary. Having made Choice 1, you can now get clear on exactly *what* is important to you. Too many see themselves as "ordinary," as cogs in a big organizational machine. They lack a clearly defined, motivating vision of the extraordinary contribution they could be making.

The truly productive don't just play the game, they change the game. They don't just do what's expected, they create their own future. They are not just "walking job descriptions," they make a unique difference that matters.

Choice 3: Schedule the Big Rocks, Don't Sort Gravel. If you've made Choice 2 and clarified the extraordinary things you want to achieve in your life, you're ready to create a plan to actually make them happen. So many live life by default. They use what energy they have on just keeping up, and they're so often frustrated at their inability to do even that. Life is just one thing after another, a stream of undifferentiated "gravel."

But this is not a picture of productivity. The truly productive actively plan how they will use their time and energy, ensuring that it goes to the "Big Rocks" rather than keeping up with the gravel.

Choice 4: Rule Your Technology, Don't Let It Rule You. Now you have your Choice 3 plan in place, but there's a problem. You can easily get blown off course by relentless demands on your time that come at you "virtually" every minute. Just when you're getting mastery over your own life, your technology threatens to master you.

Hundreds of apps are available that promise to increase productivity. Ironically, as we've seen, technology can do the opposite and disrupt productivity. Many people are "urgency addicts" who can't look up from their smartphones long enough to avoid walking into walls.

But you can leverage the same technology to become extraordinarily productive. You can design a system for yourself that keeps you focused on the important and fends off the unimportant. You can draw on the power of social media to transform your work and your life.

Choice 5: Fuel Your Fire, Don't Burn Out. You've made Choices 1 through 4. You have a new mindset, a new plan, and a new system to make it happen. But without the physical and mental energy to pursue your dreams, you risk falling victim to your own personal "energy crisis."

The crushing stress we live with can bake the brain—literally. A stressed-out brain is continually immersed in adrenaline, a high-octane chemical that overstimulates every system of the body. The result: we wear down fast, we barely get through the day, we become exhausted or even ill. And eventually, we burn out.

True productivity requires recharging the brain and body continually. People inspired by a high purpose can go far, but if they are actively caring for the brain—feeding, resting, and exercising it properly—they can go infinitely farther.

Why the 5 Choices?

In this book, we'll do a "deep dive" on each of the 5 Choices. You'll get a clear picture of what to do and the results you'll get if you make them.

Why make the 5 Choices at all?

The ability to distinguish between the important and the unimportant will be a key competency going forward in this century. Unless you can discern the Big Rocks from the gravel, you can forget about productivity. If you're obsessed with incoming gravel—whether in the form of other people's priorities or a technology addiction—you'll never be able to do the kind of reflective, strategic thinking and work that can create the future you want.

If you identify and organize yourself around your few true priorities, you'll feel more balanced, less stressed, more deeply satisfied, and more credible because you'll follow through on the most important things. You'll bypass ordinary productivity to become extraordinarily productive. That's the promise of the 5 Choices.

The principles that govern productivity never change. In fact, those principles are exponentially more relevant now as people face today's exponential increase in demands on their time. The 5 Choices are based squarely on those principles.

Every day, science reveals more about the infinitely productive capacity of the human brain—about what nourishes that capacity and what cripples it. We have interviewed the world's top brain scientists to get their best thinking on these topics. In this book, you'll read about the science behind the 5 Choices and how it can help you.

For nearly 30 years, we at FranklinCovey have led the world in helping people get the right things done. We have taught—and learned from—literally hundreds of thousands of people in more than 100 countries. Our planning system and tools have helped millions lead more fulfilling lives and achieve more fulfilling goals. We have done more research, thought harder, and shared more ideas on this topic than anyone else.

We've watched intently the revolutionary changes of our time. From listening and learning with you, we know that you have far more to do with fewer resources than ever. We know that you're buried under an avalanche of demands. We know that "insanely busy" is no joke for you. We know that the threats we've been talking about are genuine and personal to you.

We also know that deep down, you have dreams and goals. You wish you could give more of yourself to the people and causes you love. You want to make a real, substantial difference at work. You want to do extraordinary things with your one life. We know that you don't want to live, in the words of Henry David Thoreau, "a life of quiet desperation."

We know these things because you've told us—thousands of you. We've heard you. The 5 Choices are the answer.

Choice 1: Act on the Important, Don't React to the Urgent

"Anything less than a commitment to the important is a conscious commitment to the unimportant."
—*Dr. Stephen R. Covey*

How to become extraordinarily productive?

Figure out what's most important. Now give the most important things priority in your life. Everything else is secondary. Why waste your time on less important things?

It sounds so easy.

Why then is it so hard? Why do so many feel this longing to get to the most important things but can't? What's the big obstacle?

When we ask people why they have such a hard time getting organized and spending their time productively, they usually answer, "Because I have no discipline." Dr. Stephen R. Covey says this: "On deeper thought, I believe that is not the case. The basic problem is that their priorities have not become deeply planted in their hearts and minds."[8] In other words, the problem is not with what they *do* with their time, but with how they *think*.

When it comes to how to invest time, most people have one of two mindsets: *urgency* or *importance*. Whether you're operating from a mindset of urgency or a mindset of importance, it will profoundly affect your life.

The ordinary mindset is to *react* to the *urgent*—to the things that are right in front of us and "need" our immediate attention. As there is no end to these things, we believe the only way to be more productive is to try to do more things faster.

The extraordinary mindset is to *Act on the Important*— to take the initiative to determine what the *right* things are and to take action on them.

The results we get in life depend on our behavior, and our behavior depends on our mindset. What we sometimes fail to realize is that we can *choose* our mindset.

We all have a choice to make between two mental doors. Behind one of those doors is a vast universe of possibility where you—as a talented, thinking, proactive individual—can create your own future. Behind this door, you have the freedom to act on the important things in your life.

Behind the other door is a stifling mass of urgent demands on your time. Some of them are important, some not so important, but they all need your attention now! If you are a passive, reactive person, you are the victim of whatever falls on you when you open that door.

If you have the urgency mindset, your brain hovers, waiting. The email chimes, the phone buzzes, a text message beeps. There's something new. Somebody wants you. You've got to respond. Like Pavlov's famous dogs that were conditioned to salivate at the sound of a bell, you, too, have been conditioned. And if like most people you get a dozen of these little interruptions every hour—do the math—you literally can't focus on one thing for more than five minutes!

Your Brain Under Attack

"Where have all the humans gone? To their screens, of course."
—*William Powers*

What happens to your brain under the pressure of constant waves of demands, calls, emails, messages, texts, images—all of them buzzing, throbbing, and ringing all day, every day?

The brain contains both short- and long-term memory centers. Short-term memory is located in the prefrontal cortex, which acts as a gateway for the rest of the brain. All the inputs from the world outside come at you through the prefrontal cortex.

The long-term storage center of the brain contains hundreds of billions of neuron cells and another trillion star cells that connect to each other in virtually infinite ways. In fact, you have more brain cells than there are stars in our Milky Way Galaxy. Without any conscious guidance from you, this vast area of your brain miraculously regulates your balance, motion, body temperature, sight, blood pressure, and myriad other parallel processes you are not even aware of. It is a vast universe of its own.

By contrast, the prefrontal cortex—the gateway to the brain—can handle only one thing at time. Compared to the rest of the brain, the prefrontal cortex is like a teaspoon to the Milky Way.

This is why human beings find it so difficult to multitask. Physiologically, we cannot give our best conscious effort to more than one thing at a time. MIT neuroscientist Earl Miller says, "Trying to concentrate on two tasks causes an overload of the brain's processing capacity…. Particularly when people try to perform similar tasks at the same time, such as writing an email and talking on the phone, they compete to use the same part of the brain. Trying to carry too much, the brain simply slows down."

The prefrontal cortex just can't handle the daily flood that comes at us because it is designed to deal with teaspoons rather than tidal waves of information.

Constant interruptions not only slow down the brain, but also raise stress levels. Professor Gloria Mark is an "interruption scientist" at the University of California: "When people are frequently diverted from one task to another, they work faster but produce less. After 20 minutes of interrupted performance, people report significantly higher stress levels, frustration, workload, effort, and pressure."[9]

Even more worrisome, the brain that is highly fragmented and constantly interrupted may be rewiring itself in ways that make us less productive. Professor Clifford Nass of Stanford University reports that "the neural circuits devoted to scanning, skimming, and multitasking are expanding and strengthening, while those used for reading and thinking deeply, with sustained concentration, are weakening or eroding."

What's the consequence? "Habitual multitaskers may be sacrificing performance on the primary task. They are suckers for irrelevancy."

"Improving our ability to multitask actually hampers our ability to think deeply and creatively...the more you multitask, the less deliberative you become; the less able to think and reason out a problem," says Jordan Grafman of the National Institute of Neurological Disorders and Stroke in the U.S.A.[10]

Psychiatrist Ed Hallowell now sees in his practice many people who are so strung out that they suspect they are suffering from attention deficit disorder. He tells them that they actually just have a severe case of modern life. "We have been conditioned by our modern world to be in a hurry, to allow too many interruptions, to take on more than we can possibly handle, so we are developing overloaded circuits."[11]

You're addicted to urgency. A crisis comes up, you get a dopamine hit, and in time you become dependent on the rush and excitement. It gives you a temporary high until the next email hits.

On the other hand, if you proactively decide that you are in charge of your time and your life—nobody else—you begin to get the importance mindset. You don't confuse urgent things with first things. You know that just because it's urgent, it isn't necessarily important.

So everything we do falls into one of the four quadrants of this matrix.

The Time Matrix. People spend their time in one of four quadrants, depending on how urgent or important their activities are. Extraordinarily productive people try to stay in Quadrant 2.

Quadrant 1 Is the Quadrant of Necessity

Quadrant 1 things are both urgent and important. These are the things that come at you that you need to take care of *now*. That's why we call it the "Quadrant of Necessity." An angry client is on the phone, a friend has a heart attack, a key machine breaks down on the factory floor. Occasionally, a big opportunity comes up that needs attention now or it will slip away. But please notice that most of Quadrant 1 is avoidable. That client shouldn't be angry in the first place. Frankly, the friend's heart attack might be due to some lifestyle choices made long ago. That machine broke down because of a lack of maintenance.

Q1 people are urgency addicts. The gateway to the mind is crowded with critical priorities that demand attention now!

The return on your investment in Q1 is usually equal to or less than the time and energy you put into it. It's crisis management, what is often called "firefighting." Stamping out a fire might preserve something, but it produces nothing.

What is life like in Quadrant 1? It can be exciting, particularly if you're the superhero type who likes to fly in and save the day. There are people who love the rush of fighting fires; they thrive on Quadrant 1...for a while. The urgency mindset has its rewards, but they are temporary because the stress of living with incessant crises eventually burns you out.

Quadrant 3 Is the Quadrant of Distraction

Quadrant 3 things are urgent but not important. Many people spend a lot of time in Q3 thinking they're in Q1. Really, they're just reacting to other people's little emergencies. Phone calls, email, text messages, routine but empty meetings, people dropping by—all these can deceive them into thinking they're getting things done, but really they're just spinning their wheels. Meanwhile, truly important priorities fall off the agenda.

Q3 is particularly destructive because so many people confuse activity with accomplishment. It's possible to squander a lot of time in relatively useless meetings. It's possible to answer inconsequential emails and texts and social-network requests all day. A full calendar and to-do list don't necessarily add up to a full life.

Q3 people are also urgency addicts. The gateway to the mind is very crowded. Q3 has always been the true enemy of productivity—and even more so now with the technological tsunami that swamps us. As we've seen, the human brain that hovers constantly over urgencies on electronic screens is a Q3 brain.

Q3 is also the insidious home of organizational activities that lost their relevance long ago—reports that don't really need to be done, meetings no one finds terribly useful, even systems and functions that have outlived their purpose or that could be repurposed to achieve something more productive. The organizational corollary to Newton's law of inertia is "A dumb idea in motion tends to stay in motion."

Sadly, many, many people live in Q3 because they don't know what else to do. Either they can't discern what's truly important in the rush of demands on their time, or their organization has never made clear what's truly important.

The return on your investment in Q3 is always less than the time and energy you put into it because you're squandering your efforts on unimportant tasks.

What is life like in Quadrant 3? It can be comfortable and even pleasant. It's filled with rings and dings and buzzes and tweets from all the gadgets in sight. You might even be popular because you're so "responsive" to other people's priorities, even though you never get to fulfill your own. You can stay very busy doing things that don't mean much in the long run, making little difference, filling your hours with relatively pointless tasks and meetings. But in the end, it's a barren existence. As Dr. Covey asks, "How thin can you spread yourself before you're no longer there?"

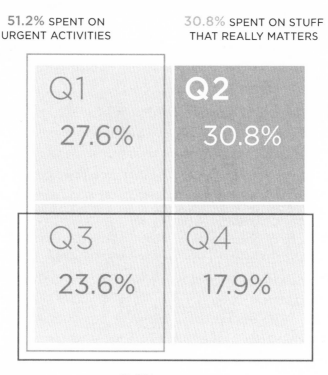

51.2% SPENT ON URGENT ACTIVITIES

30.8% SPENT ON STUFF THAT REALLY MATTERS

Q1 27.6%

Q2 30.8%

Q3 23.6%

Q4 17.9%

41.5% SPENT ON UNIMPORTANT ACTIVITIES

Where People Spend Their Time. If you're a typical worker, the three reactive Quadrants 1, 3, and 4 round up to nearly 70 percent of your work time.[12]

Quadrants 1 and 3 Are the Quadrants of Urgency

As the Time Matrix Survey shows, working people report spending *more than half of their time* (51.2 percent) in the urgency quadrants. Yet, we've seen that most of Quadrant 1 and all of Quadrant 3 is avoidable. In one alarming decade-long study, researchers examined the behavior of busy managers in nearly a dozen large companies in Europe and North America. They found that those managers squander fully 90 percent of their time in urgent but ineffective activities. They are "well-intentioned, highly energetic but unfocused people who confuse frantic motion with constructive action." And some companies actually reward the frantic activity rather than results.[13]

The real toll taken by the urgency quadrants is on your mind and heart. Because you are constantly trying to swim against a tide of crises—some significant, some trivial—you wear out and make little headway. Your potential stays untapped. As William Powers says, you get the sense that "life isn't quite hanging together, isn't adding up to what it might. It's all those unrealized epiphanies, insights and joys—journeys the mind and heart never get to take."[14]

Quadrant 4 Is the Quadrant of Waste

Quadrant 4 things are neither urgent nor important. We call this the "Quadrant of Waste" because literally nothing productive gets done. People who live in Q4 watch too much TV, spend hours and hours playing video games, surf the Internet into the early morning hours, or load trivial updates onto Facebook all day.

The human brain that hovers constantly over distractions on electronic screens is a Q4 brain, doing what William Powers calls "the digital dance…zipping from email to email to text to buzzing mobile and back again."[15]

Anything you do to excess could put you in Q4—including things that are harmless or even helpful if done in moderation, such as exercise, a movie, having a snack, or going out with friends. If you depend on Facebook to build your brand, you probably should be updating repeatedly. There's everything right with relaxing and having fun, as long as it's not excessive and motivated by a desire to evade important priorities. There's everything wrong with burning out and burning up your time with mindless entertainment.

Of course, the return on your "investment" of time and energy in Q4 is zero. You've simply exerted yourself for nothing.

What does it feel like to live in Q4? Momentary gratification, maybe; but deep down, it's all self-disgust. Many people who are burned out in the urgency quadrants end up here in the evenings to escape the stress of their daytime lives.

At a deeper level, Q4 can be the quadrant of despair. People who live in Q4 eat too much or not at all, sleep too much or not at all, party too much or withdraw into profound isolation. Emptied of purpose, they've found their way to the frayed fringes of life often because they see no meaningful alternative.

Quadrant 2 Is the Quadrant of Extraordinary Productivity

Quadrant 2 things are important but not urgent. This is the "Quadrant of Extraordinary Productivity" because here you take charge of your own life and create your own great future. Q2 people do the thoughtful, creative, proactive work that changes the world. They act on the important; they don't react to the urgent. They plan, they prepare, they prevent crises. They learn, they create, they build relationships. They continually renew their energy levels so they don't burn out. They do the things everyone knows are most important but few seem to get to.

The return on your investment in Q2 is always more—often exponentially more—than the time and energy you put into it. Ten minutes to plan your day can make the other 23 hours and 50 minutes much more productive. A quick read of the latest journal in your field can put you far ahead of others in a meeting. And an afternoon's outing with your little daughter—just the two of you—can create a lifelong bond.

The importance of moving to Quadrant 2 can't be overemphasized. This is the quadrant of proactivity; the others are quadrants of reactivity where the passive, primitive part of the brain takes over. One corporate leader admits that he devotes very little of his time to being proactive. "The rest of my life, and I would suggest most people's lives, is spent in some sort of daily daze, reading emails, getting stuck in traffic and going to meetings that are in some ways diversions.... And the long-term goals that stand in front of me suddenly become impossible tasks that can't be tackled now."[16] Reactivity is hardwired into his brain; challenges that require proactivity seem insurmountable to him.

When we live in Q2, we engage the sophisticated executive center of the brain, the frontal lobes of the neocortex. "The frontal lobes are to the brain what a conductor is to an orchestra, a general to an army, the chief executive officer to a corporation. [They are] the brain's command post."[17] The more Q2 choices we consciously make, the more we rewire the executive brain to respond proactively.

That's because each Q2 choice we make strengthens the proactive brain and suppresses the reactive brain, which is associated with the limbic system. Our reflexes are centered in this more primitive part of the brain—any external stimulus prods it into action, such as a loud noise, a sudden threat, or even the bell on your computer announcing an incoming email. According to the prominent brain scientist and author Richard Restak:

"The prefrontal lobes are the seat of maturity, judgment, emotional control, decision making, planning, etc. They are also under attack. The characteristic of the adult brain is the ability to override the limbic system with the frontal lobes; that is, to make a conscious choice. It is this capability that allows us to control our lives and create the results we want, instead of simply being at the mercy of external stimuli."[18]

How does it feel to live in Q2? Some of the words we've heard: "fulfilled, at peace, energized, in control." People who live in Q2 are the highly effective people Stephen R. Covey talks about. They habitually Put First Things First in their lives. They do most of the truly productive work in the world. They transcend the ordinary and live extraordinary lives. They don't just get things done—they get the *right* things done.

Living in Q2

*"Effective people stay out of Quadrants 3 and 4 because,
urgent or not, they aren't important. They also shrink Quadrant 1
down to size by spending more time in Quadrant 2.
Quadrant 2 is the heart of effective personal management."*
— Stephen R. Covey

Now you should see more clearly how to Put First Things First in your life:

- Get out of Q3 and Q4 entirely. Nothing below that midline is important. No one should have to live a life of distraction or despair.

- Visit Q1 only when you must. Too much time in Q1 burns you out because it's mostly managing crises you could prevent if you spent more time in Q2.

- Move to Q2—permanently.

But why should you want to move to Q2? Doesn't it mean more work? more effort? Does it mean you have to do more with less?

No, paradoxically—just the opposite. Let's dive a little deeper into the transformation that takes place when you move to Q2.

From Reactive to Proactive. Q2 people don't play the victim. They don't much believe in the power of circumstances to control their lives. Instead, they believe in their own power to *transform* their lives. They see themselves not as passive functionaries, but as high-value contributors.

From Crisis Manager to Crisis Preventer. Q2 people know that the cheapest problem to solve is the one they never have in the first place, so they anticipate, plan for, and prevent Q1 emergencies. Instead of fighting fires, they prevent fires. The more Q2 grows, the more Q1 shrinks.

From Imbalanced to Balanced. Q2 people balance the crucial roles they play in life. Unlike the hyperbusy, out-of-control people in the "urgency" column ("Someday when I get a chance, I'll spend some quality time with my friend/my spouse/my child/my friend/my mother"), they invest deeply in building those precious relationships. Instead of neglecting their own well-being ("I just don't have time to exercise"), they regularly renew and recharge themselves.

From Distracted to Focused. They refuse to be constantly distracted by beeping laptops, throbbing texts, and singing ringtones that steal their focus. Instead, they *leverage* the marvelous high-tech tools that enable great productivity. They use these tools strategically to fend off distractions and to sharpen their focus on what matters.

From Burned Out to Fired Up. Q2 people focus their finest attention and effort on things that really matter to them, that arise from the organization's highest priorities and from their own hearts and minds. These priorities derive from strategic plans, organizational and personal mission statements, visions of a better future, and goals that inspire. Excited people work hard but are not burnouts.

So, what's a Quadrant 2 day like?

You get a little exercise in the morning, maybe a refreshing walk; eat a sensible breakfast. On the job, you tackle the most important things first, the things that will make the most difference *over time*, instead of getting buried in a pile of email. You have lunch with real people instead of your laptop, so you feed the relationships you value. After work, you reconnect with your loved ones—watch some fun TV or play a game. And all this time, you're working toward goals that have real meaning for you.

The alternative is to live in the other quadrants. No time for exercise in the morning. Grab coffee. Dive into your email and consume your day answering other people's urgencies—some important, some not. This "work" piles up, so you can't take time for lunch—only caffeine keeps you going. Work late and go home exhausted to an equally exhausted family. You're so wired up, you can't sleep, so you burn up the night in Quadrant 4, surfing the Internet or TV or gaming. The next day, it starts over. Though you're incredibly tired and busy, you never feel like you're accomplishing anything meaningful.

So where would you rather live—in Quadrant 2, or in the other quadrants? Have you ever worked with someone who is a crisis manager, out of balance, reactive, distracted, burned out, or just playing the game? Have you ever *been* that person?

But if you were a crisis preventer, a planner, proactive, well balanced, focused, fired up, and actively changing the game, wouldn't your life be qualitatively different?

Think about the consequences of neglecting Q2, as so many are doing more and more in this distracted age. In the end, if you haven't chosen to live in Q2, it won't matter which other quadrants you choose to live in.

At the age of 26, within the space of what is called his "miracle year," Albert Einstein published three scientific papers that transformed our understanding of the universe. In these papers, he set out the laws of relativity that govern time and space and the power of the atom.

His ideas arose during long hours of what most people would call daydreaming, in which he did his "thought experiments." He knew that riding up in an elevator makes you heavier—what would happen, he asked himself, if that elevator were to accelerate infinitely. Would you become infinitely heavy? He thought about traveling on a light ray. He contemplated why train whistles change tune just as they pass. He wondered what matter really is, and why there is energy in the universe.

What would a 26-year-old Einstein be doing if he lived in our noisy, attention-deficit 21st century? Would he be dreaming about what it would be like to ride on a beam of light? Or would he be updating his Facebook status for the 13th time today?

Quadrant 2 Versus "Time Management"

Isn't it obvious that Q2 is the best mindset to have and the best place to be? Then why don't more people move there? Why, according to our decades of research, do people spend on the average less than a third of their time in Q2?

The strong psychological barrier to Q2 is the urgency mindset, which assumes that the key to productivity is getting things done. There are so many things to do and, as we say, they all needed to be done yesterday. People goad themselves, "If only I could get to everything." They suppose that the more stuff they get done, the more productive they are.

This urgency mindset has given rise to an industry called "time management." We see an explosion of productivity tools and apps, all of which claim to help you get more things done. They teach you how to make a to-do list and to schedule everything and sync it all up and talk about how fulfilling it is to check everything off your to-do list.

But as we have seen, this mindset is crippling. The key to true productivity is not to get things done, but to get the right things done—the important things. In fact, the key to extraordinary productivity is to do not more *with* less, but more *about* less—about those few priorities that really matter.

As Dr. Covey has said, "It's possible to be very busy and not very effective. You have to decide what your highest priorities are and have the courage—pleasantly, smilingly, nonapologetically—to say no to other things. And the way you do that is by having a bigger 'yes' burning inside."[19]

"Time management" is really a misnomer. The challenge is not to manage time, but to change mindsets—to move into Q2 where you can transform your life, where the "burning yes" resides.

Create a Q2 Culture

Now you say, "I'd be glad to move into Quadrant 2 if other people would let me. But in my company, everything is a Quadrant 1 priority. Everything's important and everything has to be done now—or even better, yesterday!"

It's tough to move to Quadrant 2 if no one else comes with you. That's why you'll want to start building a Q2 culture around yourself. If you think Q2 is a great place to live, you can be sure others will too.

We all have a culture—up, down, or sideways, even if it's just you and your boss or you and a co-worker.

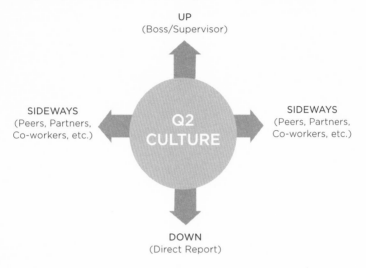

Q2 Culture. You are at the center of your own culture, which radiates out from you to your boss, peers, co-workers, direct reports, and so forth. You can influence this culture to move into Quadrant 2.

Is the culture you live in a Quadrant 2 culture? Probably not. But if you do a few simple things, you'll gradually see a change in the culture around you.

First, see yourself as a teacher and start spreading the word about Quadrant 2. The key is to share your understanding of the Time Matrix among the people around you.

Sit down with your boss and co-workers and sketch the Time Matrix for them. Ask which tasks, projects, or other activities belong in which quadrant. This should be a significant "aha!" for them as they begin to realize how much time they're spending on less important activities.

Soon you'll hear people using a common language:

"Is this a Q1? Do I need to do it right now?"

"Is this a Q3? Do we really need to do this at all?"

"I think I'm in Q4. What can I do to change?"

"This is a Q2 priority. We need to spend our time on this."

This common language helps people judge how much effort to invest in a task. When you see people emailing each other saying, "This is a genuine Q1," you'll know the culture is starting to change.

The hardest part of saying yes to Q2 is saying no to everything else. When someone comes at you with a request to do something less important, you should be able to say no courteously and serenely because of the "deeper yes" burning inside of you. Still, you don't want to disregard people and their needs.

If you really want to be extraordinarily productive, you don't just surrender to every demand on your time. In the moment of choice, you pause, clarify the request, and decide based on the Time Matrix what to do about it.

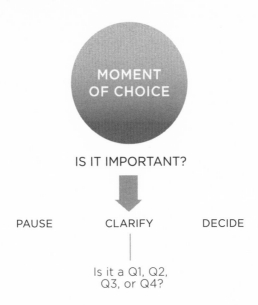

When to Say No. When faced with a choice on how to spend your time, pause and clarify which quadrant you're in. If the request is below the midline, you should say no to it.

Ask yourself, "Is this request a Q1 or a Q2?" If so, you need to act on it because it truly is important. "Is it a Q3 or a Q4?" If so, find a diplomatic way to say no:

"Is there someone else who could take that on?"

"I've got an important deadline to meet. Can we talk about that tomorrow?" (Usually, if it's a Q3 request, it will take care of itself long before tomorrow comes.)

"Let's schedule a time when I can show you how to do this yourself."

"I wish I could help, but I won't be able to, given the other priorities I have right now."

The more you say no, the more time you'll have for the yes—the true priorities of Quadrant 2. You'll get used to it, and others will learn that you live in Q2.

If you teach others about the Time Matrix and practice what you teach, you will be creating a Q2 culture around yourself. Everything starts with you, and there's the catch.

In a way, it's easier to just default to the urgency mindset. Everything's important. Everything's urgent. Whatever needs to be done, you do it. You schedule it and follow through. You take care of business. Everyone thinks of you as a good time manager. You're even popular because of it. You're a "people pleaser." They all know they can count on good old you.

But it takes initiative from deep inside yourself to focus on important things that aren't urgent. You *react* to the urgent, but in Q2, you have to act to make important things happen. Nothing in Q2 comes at you—you come at Q2. You have a proactive mentality. You're firm about the "few and the true" priorities that will make the most difference. You might be less popular with some people because you say no a lot, but the "yes" is worth it.

In other words, to move to Quadrant 2 takes a conscious choice. That's why it's the first of the 5 Choices. The other four provide you with the process and tools that will help you move to Q2 and stay there. But unless you make Choice 1, the others don't mean much.

Think about it this way: You're moving to a beautiful new home, the place you really want to be. Of course, moving can be messy and challenging at first, but the destination makes all the difference. The 5 Choices will get you to that destination.

Teach to Learn

The best way to learn is to teach. Use the Time Matrix below to teach others about the mindset of extraordinary productivity.

Q1 NECESSITY

Crises
Emergency meetings
Last-minute deadlines
Pressing problems
Unforeseen events

Q2 EXTRAORDINARY PRODUCTIVITY

Proactive work
High-impact goals
Creative thinking
Planning
Prevention
Relationship building
Learning and renewal

Q3 DISTRACTION

Needless interruptions
Unnecessary reports
Irrelevant meetings
Other people's minor issues
Unimportant email, tasks, phone
  calls, status posts, etc.

Q4 WASTE

Trivial work
Avoidance activities
Excessive relaxation, television,
  gaming, Internet
Time-wasters
Gossip

IMPORTANT

NOT IMPORTANT

URGENT ◀━━━━━━━━━━━━━━━━━▶ NOT URGENT

Choice 2: Go for Extraordinary, Don't Settle for Ordinary

"Every life has the potential to be lived deeply."
—William Powers

You've made Choice 1: Act on the Important. You're determined to move into the quadrant of extraordinary productivity. Like the brave ant in the picture, you're not going to carry crumbs all your life. You're going to carry the strawberry.

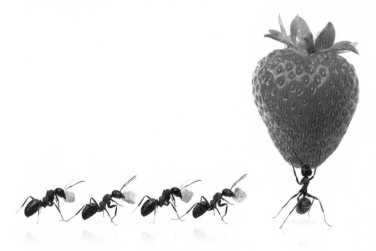

Choice 2 is about "getting clear on the strawberry"—on what is most important to you. When you really examine your heart and mind, you get down to the few things that really matter to you and deserve your best and finest effort.

People with the ordinary mindset tend to do what's expected of them and no more. Doing what's expected takes enough out of them as it is. Why do more than that?

As we've said, it's not a question of doing more, but of doing less—less of the merely expected and more of the truly remarkable. People with the mindset of going for the extraordinary carry as few crumbs as possible. They know exactly what their top priorities are and focus their strength on them.

Put simply, Choice 2 is to clearly define those most important priorities. This exercise provides clarity to a brain that is fogged up by a multiplicity of distractions. Dr. Daniel G. Amen told us: "To harness your brain's power, it needs direction and vision. It needs a blueprint. You are more likely to be successful if you define success clearly, specifically, in writing, with detail."[20]

You will be living by design, not by default.

Making Choice 2 keeps you on the path toward extraordinary productivity rather than the path of "settling," which leads you to being buried alive under the weight of conflicting demands.

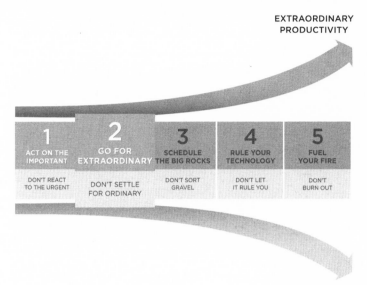

EXTRAORDINARY
PRODUCTIVITY

1	2	3	4	5
ACT ON THE IMPORTANT	GO FOR EXTRAORDINARY	SCHEDULE THE BIG ROCKS	RULE YOUR TECHNOLOGY	FUEL YOUR FIRE
DON'T REACT TO THE URGENT	DON'T SETTLE FOR ORDINARY	DON'T SORT GRAVEL	DON'T LET IT RULE YOU	DON'T BURN OUT

BURIED ALIVE

As we've seen, organizing your life around your most important priorities is the key to extraordinary productivity. But what are your Quadrant 2 priorities? Where do they come from?

We constantly hear people talk about their highest priorities and the anxiety they feel at being unable to get to them. "I want to make a difference at work, but I don't seem to be able to get there, no matter how much effort I make. And in my company, you're a slacker if you're not the first in every morning and the last to leave at night. I get home late. I have no time or energy for family or friends. There's no time for games or films or concerts, no chance to just talk. Everybody else is strung out too. I'd like to get to know the neighbors, connect with my old friends, help out in the community. And exercise? There's just no time."

Identify the Key Roles in Your Life

Ultimately, your highest priorities come from your deepest self—from who you *are*. And you are actually *many* different selves. You might be an engineer or a lawyer or a teacher. More than that, you're also someone's child or brother or wife or mother. You're also a thinking member of society, a citizen, a helper, a learner, a friend. And maybe you're a musician or a scholar or an athlete. All of these roles are important to you; they make you who you are.

When we speak of the roles you play, we are not talking about ordinary roles defined by your gender or function or the expectations others have of you. We're talking about Quadrant 2 Roles defined by what's important to you at a fundamental level—by the impact you have in those roles on your own life and on the lives of those around you. Your most basic values derive from your Q2 Roles.

Here's what we mean by the radical difference between a functional role and a Q2 Role.

Functional Role	Q2 Role
Accountant	Investment Maximizer
Father	Dad
Director	Catalyst for Change
Banker	Small-Business Promoter
Grandparent	Greatest Fan

What's the difference between "I'm an accountant" and "I maximize the value of investments for my company"? A functional role is just mechanical, whereas a Q2 Role is about making a difference that energizes and rewards you and those who depend on you. Any man can be a father; but there's all the difference in the world between a *father* and a *dad*.

Moving mentally into Quadrant 2 means that you fundamentally change how you see your roles in your personal life and on the job. Now you say, "But I can't redefine my work role. It's already been defined in my job description."

If you are simply working as a job description, you're deep into a reactive mindset. A job description isn't very different from an instruction book for putting a machine together. But you are not a machine. You're a thinking, talented, unique human being with extraordinary things to do. Instead of passively doing what's expected, reset your brain: "What does my job really require from me? What contribution can I make here that no one else could make?"

Instead of tackling whatever job is expected of you, start asking why you should do this job in the first place. This is the great Q2 question.

A college student who needed money went to work on a telephone help desk for a large online retailer. His role? Customer-service representative. It came with a perfunctory job description. After 15 minutes of training, he put on a telephone headset, clicked on his computer screen, and took his first call: "I'm so sorry you received the wrong product. Let me help you with that." Thirty more calls that first afternoon convinced him the world was full of cranky people.

One day between calls, he got up to stretch his legs and walked around the call center. He counted 200 people just like himself, all of them chatting with irritated people. Idly, he did a few mental calculations. If all these people made the same salary he did, the company was spending two or three million a year on this operation.

But then he thought, "Why do they spend all this money fixing problems that never should have happened in the first place?"

The question bothered him. He started writing down the reasons for the calls he got, and soon saw patterns in these complaints. He realized that if the shipping department just did a couple of things differently—fairly simple things—many of his calls would go away. They could easily prevent these problems.

So he decided to talk it over with his manager, who was smart enough to take the idea seriously. Soon the volume of complaints dropped. And the former customer-service representative, whose job had been to fix problems, now saw himself in a new Q2 Role: "Customer Problem Preventer." Once he got clear on the contribution he could make, extraordinary things happened.

He shifted from an ordinary mindset to an extraordinary mindset in these ways:

Ordinary	Extraordinary
Function	Contribution
Tasks	Outcomes
Low Impact	High Impact
Play the Game	Change the Game
Disengaged	Engaged

He no longer saw himself in terms of his function as an interchangeable part of a machine. No longer passive and reactive, he now saw himself in terms of the proactive contribution he could make.

Instead of settling for doing the tasks he was assigned to do, he began to think in terms of outcomes that were truly important to the organization. In other words, he became clear on the "job to be done." Supposedly, his job consisted of answering ringing phones, an urgency role if there ever was one—*or so it seemed*. But that wasn't really his job at all! It was only a means to doing his *real* job, which was to build loyalty among the firm's customers.

Rather than squander his energies in low-impact work, he chose to invest his energies in high-impact work that would actually make a measurably important difference to the company's balance sheet. The company not only wasted less money on rework, but they earned more business from more loyal customers.

So many ordinary people just "play the game." He chose to *change* the game. So many just accept the rules as a given without actually employing their own brains and asking themselves, "Is there a better way to win this game?"

Finally, he went from being disengaged in the work—it was just a means to an end, a way to get tuition money for college—to being mentally and emotionally engaged in solving an important problem. There is a world of difference between an engaged and a disengaged brain.

Now, remember that this young man was a college student with no training, in an entry-level job with no career track at all. His example illustrates the power of a Q2 mindset. It shows that any role—no matter how menial—can become transformative.

Your Q2 Roles:

- Represent your true responsibilities and relationships.

- Express your deepest values, highest aspirations, and greatest contributions.

- Give a balanced perspective to your life.

- Should be limited to a few (five to seven).

Q2 Roles are the sources of meaning for you. You don't really understand the meaning of parenthood until you become a parent. You don't really grasp what it means to be a doctor or a soldier or a scientist until you become one. You might like music, but you don't really feel what it is to make music unless you're a musician.

Q2 Roles are also the source of balance. Your Q2 Roles add up to your whole life—your heart, mind, body, and soul. You have roles defined by relationships that fill your heart; your mind is engaged in your work;

your body needs constant renewal and recharging; and your soul needs meaning and purpose. A balanced life requires attention to each of these roles. An imbalanced life loses track of them.

Most important, a Q2 Role is actually a vision of an extraordinary contribution you could make. In his book *Hamlet's BlackBerry*, William Powers makes this profound observation:

"Great artists, thinkers, and leaders all have an unusual capacity to be 'grasped' by some idea or mission, an inner engagement that drives them to pursue a vision, undaunted by obstacles. Beethoven, Michelangelo, Emily Dickinson, Einstein, Martin Luther King—we call them 'brilliant,' as if it were pure intelligence that made them who they were. But what unites them is what they *did* with their intelligence, the depth they reached in their thinking and brought to bear in their work."[21]

When you are truly "grasped" by your roles—as a creator, a nurturer, a learner, an agent for change, or whatever it might be—you move into a Quadrant 2 mindset. What you *do* with that role is the very definition of extraordinary productivity.

Craft Q2 Role Statements

Moving into Q2 means redefining the roles you play in life as Q2 Roles. You do this by crafting a Q2 Role Statement that renames the role and defines what success looks like in the role.

For example, what if a teacher reformulated his or her role as "learning coach"? That view of success might change radically from "covering the subject" to "enabling students to become lifetime learners."

What if a grandmother—a natural role—redefined herself as "my grandson's greatest fan"? Her vision of success in that role would take on a fundamentally different character.

One of the most inspirational things you will ever do is to craft a Quadrant 2 Role Statement that sums up what that role in life really means to you and what you want to achieve in that role.

AS... (ROLE TITLE)   I WILL... (EXTRAORDINARY OUTCOMES)   THROUGH... (ACTIVITIES)

Here's the formula for crafting a Q2 Role Statement:

1. Start by retitling your role. You're not just a product developer, you're a "Thought Leader." You're not just a salesperson, you're a "Customer Problem Solver." You're not just a runner, you're a "Human Bullet"! Give your role a title that sums up the extraordinary thing you do in that role.

2. Explain simply and clearly the extraordinary outcomes you will achieve in that role. "As a Customer Problem Solver, I will connect my customers with solutions that fit them exactly." "As a Thought Leader, I will help my company gain worldwide influence." "As a Human Bullet, I will be a top competitor in every race I enter."

3. Explain briefly how you will achieve those

outcomes. "As a Customer Problem Solver, I will connect my customers with solutions that fit them exactly, through tailoring current products or creating new ones." "As a Thought Leader, I will help my company gain worldwide influence through well-researched and carefully crafted products." "As a Human Bullet, I will be a top competitor in every race through off-road and high-intensity hill workouts." This step gives your Q2 Role Statement specificity as you define the action you will take to realize your role.

To help you craft this statement, ask yourself questions like these:

"What do I see myself doing and achieving in this role?"

"Who are the people I most influence when I'm in this role?"

"What would I want those people to say about me in this role?"

A Q2 Role Statement transforms your mindset and expresses the value, contribution, and difference you want to make in the world. So give some thoughtful attention to crafting your Q2 Role Statements.

Set Q2 Goals

In your Q2 Role Statement, you've defined a vision of success. Now sit down and define the specific actions you'll take to achieve that vision. We call these your Q2 Goals.

Many people resist this step. They don't want to be "tied down" by anything like a Q2 Goal. They want to be "free." They're happy just "doing their best." Brain science, however, tells us that ambitious, well-defined goals are essential to extraordinary productivity:

"Evidence from more than 1,000 studies conducted by researchers across the globe shows that goals that not only spell out *exactly* what needs to be accomplished, but that also set the bar for achievement *high*, result in far superior performance than simply trying to 'do your best.' That's because more difficult goals cause you to, often unconsciously, increase your effort, focus, and commitment to the goal, persist longer, and make better use of the most effective strategies."[22]

A Q2 Goal is not a casual goal. That's why you'll want to define it very specifically in these terms: "From X to Y by When."

- "I will go from 220 pounds to 180 pounds by July 1."

- "I will reduce customer complaints from 700 a week to 150 a week by the end of the fiscal year."

- "I will launch a marketing campaign that will increase revenues to our division from $1.3 million to $1.6 million by the end of the third quarter."

Of course, you don't have to be rigid about this. With some goals, the "X to Y by When" is implied:

- "I will complete leader certification by September 30."

- "I will capture at least five good leads per week this quarter."

- "I will make personal contact with each of my grandchildren this summer."

The Q2 Role Statement for our young customer-service representative might look like this:

"As a Customer Problem Preventer, I significantly increase customer loyalty through identifying patterns of problems and ways to stop them from happening."

Then he would ask himself, "How can I carry this role forward?"

He would make goals—actual numerical goals—to reduce the volume of complaints. After studying the issue, he found that most complaints arose over misdirected shipments and credit-card charges. He found that the company took 732 calls each week about shipment problems. In consulting with the shipping department, he figured that about 150 of those calls were due to a simple scheduling issue that could be fixed.

He also found that many resellers were getting their credit-card orders questioned simply because they didn't fill out the orders properly. He took on the job of tutoring them.

So his goals looked like this:

- "Reduce calls about misdirected shipments by 20 percent by year end."

- "Tutor every reseller in the system on the proper way to fill out credit-card orders by year end."

In tracking his progress on these goals, he paid close attention to the patterns of complaints and continued to get to the root of the customers' problems. Winning at this game excited him. Sure enough, complaints went down and customer-loyalty scores went up.

Note that he set only a couple of Q2 Goals. The more goals you set, the less likely you are to achieve them with excellence. Remember, the principle is to focus your finest attention and effort on the "few and the true" priorities.

Your roles and goals will change with different seasons of your life. You get a new job. You go back to school. You sign up for a community project. The birth of your child means you take on a thoroughly new, profoundly meaningful role. And with the change in roles will come a change in goals.

That's why you should revisit your Q2 Roles and Goals periodically—at least once a year. You might have entirely different roles this year, or you might make minor changes or no changes at all in how you formulate your roles and goals.

At the beginning of the year, transfer your Q2 Roles and Goals into your personal-management tool so you can easily revisit your record of what you want to achieve.

And remember that your Q2 Goals are the only ones truly worth pursuing. They enable you to realize your vision of an extraordinarily life.

Teach to Learn

The best way to learn is to teach. Use the tool below to teach others why and how to craft Q2 Roles and Goals.

Q2 ROLES AND GOALS STATEMENTS

ROLE   TITLE

_____

STATEMENT

_____

_____

_____

GOAL(S)   _____

_____

_____

_____

ROLE   TITLE

_____

STATEMENT

_____

_____

_____

GOAL(S)   _____

_____

_____

_____

Choice 3: Schedule the Big Rocks, Don't Sort Gravel

"What's at stake is the important things we could be accomplishing in our work and in our lives and our ability to enjoy them. This is a function of our ability to discern what really matters and act in productive ways to carry these things out in our lives."
— Dr. Richard Restak

True productivity, as we've seen, requires a shift to the Q2 mindset.

We can illustrate this shift by visualizing a pile of big rocks next to a pile of gravel. The big rocks represent truly important priorities that are not urgent. The gravel represents everything else. Next to these two piles is an empty jar that represents the amount of time ahead of you.

The question: What will you put into the jar first?

It all depends on your mindset.

If you have the urgency mindset, you pour the gravel in first. Why? Because you have to take care of all the urgent gravel first before you can turn your attention to the big rocks. They aren't urgent, see? The problem is, when you try to put the big rocks into the jar, there isn't enough room. It's full of gravel. So the truly important priorities, perversely, always take second place to less important things.

But if you have the Q2 mindset, what do you do? You put the big rocks into the jar first and then add gravel. If there isn't enough room for all the gravel, it doesn't matter much.

This is why Choice 3 is Schedule the Big Rocks, Don't Sort Gravel.

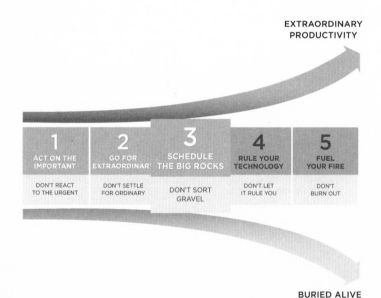

Now that you've made Choices 1 and 2, you've decided what "extraordinary productivity" means for you—it's summed up in your Q2 Roles and Goals. By making Choice 3, you organize your life around those "few and true" roles and goals.

Choice 3 is to put the Big Rocks—those activities that will enable you to achieve your Q2 Roles and Goals—into the jar before you add the gravel.

Nevertheless, we understand that it's not that simple. We know how hard it is to move to Q2 because the gravel doesn't just disappear if you ignore it. Besides, although the gravel might be relatively inconsequential, a lot of it still needs to be done.

The key is to develop the Quadrant 2 Planning habit. People with the ordinary mindset "don't have time to plan. Things are moving so fast, it's pointless to make plans. You have to take things as they come." These people are so busy driving, they don't have time to consult the map. Although they have no idea where they are, they burn a lot of fuel and cover a lot of ground, so they must be making progress, right?

By contrast, extraordinarily productive people do Quadrant 2 Planning. They have a clear vision of their key roles and the extraordinary goals they want to achieve within those roles. They map out the course to that destination. They frequently and regularly check the map to ensure they're following that straight course toward their goals. They are careful about planning for the journey. They can't afford not to plan.

That's why the following Q2 Planning process will help you, as Stephen R. Covey says, "keep the main thing the main thing."

1. Create a Master Task List.

2. Do Weekly Q2 Planning.

3. Do Daily Q2 Planning.

1. Create a Master Task List

Most of us have a big pile of mental gravel: email inboxes, a stack of papers that need attention, a to-do list, a social-media page that cries out for updating, phone calls to return, people to get back to. The pile grows every second.

Many people spend hours a day just trying to manage all this mental gravel. When we ask people what's in the pile, they admit that most of it is Q3 stuff. But it weighs on them. To get to Q2, it helps to clear the path of all this gravel and then systematically manage it so it doesn't pile up again.

You do this by creating a Master Task List. Use paper or go to the task bar on your computer and record everything you need to do in the upcoming week—tasks, errands, appointments and calls you should make, messages you should send, and so forth.

Then review your Q2 Roles and Goals. Circle everything on your Master Task List that advances those roles and goals. These are Big Rocks. Everything else is gravel.

Keep your Master Task List in a notebook or a task application so you can review it regularly.

2. Do Weekly Q2 Planning

Now, at the beginning of each week, find a quiet place to do about a half hour's Q2 Planning for that week. It's called Q2 Planning because you are focusing on:

- Proactive things to do to advance your roles and goals.

- Creative thinking.

- Crisis prevention.

- Building relationships.

- Learning and renewal.

The setting is important. Brain scientists agree that getting away, disconnecting from the noise, is essential to this kind of higher-level thinking. Psychologist Dr. Heidi Halvorson reports that "when people engage in the right kind of planning, their success rates go up on average between 200 and 300 percent."[23] Your Weekly Q2 Planning time is a classic Q2 priority.

Why do Weekly Q2 Planning? Because the week is a manageable unit of time. Business offices, schools, and other organizations generally operate within the framework of the week, designating some days for business and others for relaxation or inspiration. It's easier to "get your head around" a week than, say, a quarter or a month.

TAKE AT LEAST **30** MINUTES TO...

Weekly Q2 Planning Process. Start by reviewing your Q2 Roles and Goals. From these, you'll derive tasks that will help you advance those goals—these are the Big Rocks that go into your schedule first. Then organize everything else around the Big Rocks.

1. Connect with your Q2 Roles and Goals and your Master Task List. Review them and remind yourself why you wrote them. For each of your Q2 Roles, ask yourself this question: "What are the one or two **most important** things I can do this week that will have the most impact on fulfilling this role?" The answers to this question are your Big Rocks for the week.

2. Assign them to your schedule.

3. Organize the rest—fill your schedule in with gravel, if you choose.

Now, it's important to be realistic. Just because you begin your week with a great plan doesn't mean the week will cooperate.

A good sports team will always plan some plays and practice them hard. They might even perfect a few plays. But as soon as the game begins, the odds are pretty high that things won't go as planned. Does that mean the team shouldn't plan at all? No, because the odds are also high that the game will go better with planning than without it.

Weekly Q2 Planning is about creating the perfect "play" for the week, so you have a benchmark for making decisions. Otherwise, you could slip back into the urgency mindset and helplessly react to what comes at you.

In your planning session, keep your focus on your Q2 Roles and Goals. No gravel can be allowed to displace them. Without Q2 Roles and Goals, we are likely to slip back into the urgency mindset. As Robert A. Heinlein has said, "In the absence of clearly defined goals, we become strangely loyal to performing daily acts of trivia until ultimately we become enslaved by it."

Asking the question "What are the one or two **most important** things I can do in this role this week?" helps you to keep that focus.

Some Big Rocks become permanent fixtures of your calendar. You set aside "Q2 Time Zones" for them because they recur weekly or daily. For example, the "Customer Problem Preventer" in the customer-service center had a goal to reduce shipment complaints by 20 percent. To achieve that goal, he had several tasks to do. Each day he would sort his calls by category, so he set up a 15-minute time zone for that task at the end of each shift. He scheduled another time zone for regular meetings with his manager to review his findings. He designated a time zone for writing scripts to try out on customers.

Some weeks he discovered other Big Rock tasks. Once he identified credit-card mistakes as a key problem, he set himself the task to study the system for taking credit cards to see where mistakes could be prevented. This task required a certain amount of time each day for several weeks.

Those tasks he had no time for he entered into his Master Task List for future scheduling.

Thirty minutes a week for Weekly Q2 Planning will transform the week.

3. Do Daily Q2 Planning

Now find 10 minutes a day to do Q2 Planning for the next day. In a quiet place, close out your day. Review your tasks and appointments. "Capture the gold" from the day—insights, questions, decisions, or milestones you want to keep a record of. Identify your "must-dos" for tomorrow—your Big Rocks and any Q1 priorities that come at you. Make sure your plan is realistic: don't overplan a day that's already full.

TAKE AT LEAST **10** MINUTES TO...

Daily Q2 Planning Process. At the end of the day, take 10 minutes to close out your day by reviewing events and noting important things you want to remember. Then identify your "must-dos" for the next day and organize other tasks around the must-dos.

Weekly and Daily Q2 Planning are essential to staying in Q2. The few minutes you invest in Q2 Planning each week and each day will pay dividends as you see your most important goals being achieved.

Although this process might seem routine, it's important to recognize what's happening to your brain as you develop the Q2 Planning habit. According to Harvard brain scientists Jeff Brown and Mark Fenske, as you "frame ordinary tasks in terms of the positive outcomes they produce," the brain produces more dopamine, which plays a key role in motivating you to do them. Certain brain regions "kick into gear to move you from intention to action."

"To the extent that you can find a way to feel inspired by the everyday tasks essential to reaching your goal, the more likely you are to complete the goal. Feeling the reward in everyday activities is important, especially when goal attainment is a long way off, as with academic and career aspirations."[24]

Because you repeatedly connect to your Q2 Roles and Goals, each day becomes imbued with meaning and purpose. You feel like each task carries you toward an important end. Your chances of achieving something extraordinary increase.

The 30/10 Promise

Here's a promise. If you will spend 30 minutes a week and 10 minutes a day doing Q2 Planning, your entire week will be transformed.

Now you've made this great plan and a new day begins. Then the phone rings. An email arrives. Somebody's standing at your office door. The boss wants to see you. Each moment presents a new challenge to your Q2 resolve. Sometimes the whole universe seems to be conspiring to drag you back into the urgency mentality.

In that moment of choice, pause, clarify the importance of this new demand, then decide. Don't just reflexively surrender to the urgent, or your Q2 vision is doomed.

What are the scenarios that hit you broadside? What are the challenges you face that can wrench you away from your Q2 agenda?

Whatever they are, remember *you always have a choice.* You can choose urgency, or you can choose Q2 (which you will do if you consider the consequences). If so, eventually you become so adept in this mindset that you reflexively choose Q2 in the moment of distraction or interruption. The 30/10 Promise will be fulfilled. And your life and work will be transformed.

Teach to Learn

The best way to learn is to teach. Use the process map below to teach others why and how to do Q2 Planning.

IS IT IMPORTANT?
(PAUSE, CLARIFY, DECIDE)

Choice 4: Rule Your Technology, Don't Let It Rule You

"A real challenge in everyday life is the continual push-pull, the friction between the external world trying to capture your attention and the internal world where you focus on achieving your most important goals."
— *Dr. Edward Vogel*

Possibly, the most significant threat to your productivity is the very technology designed to accelerate it —your smartphone, your laptop, your tablet, your television.

We all know people who believe that if they could just get the latest and greatest gadgetry, they would become heroically productive. This is usually a fantasy. They think it will save them from the hard work of running their own lives.

Then there are people who are slaves to texting, tweeting, messaging, and mailing—and they enjoy their servitude. Captivated by their tools, they rarely look up from them. Clearly, this is not the route to extraordinary productivity; still, most of us are hooked to one degree or another.

According to eminent clinical psychologist Kathleen Nadeau, "We can start craving overload. The same brain circuitry that is involved in other addictions is also involved in technology addiction." But there is good news too.

"We can rewire our brains. We can develop habits of thought that keep us in charge, that help us maximize the conscious mind so that we do not literally lose ourselves in a storm of distractions."[25]

Extraordinarily productive people choose to leverage technology rather than let it rule their lives. Choice 4 is Rule Your Technology, Don't Let It Rule You.

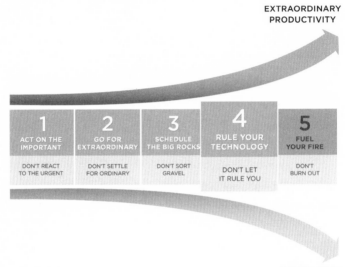

By making Choices 1 through 3, you have a clear view of the extraordinary things you want to accomplish. But having made these choices, you still face a serious hazard from incoming disruption—the more than 100 trillion emails sent each year all seem addressed to you. The electronic blizzard you face can blind you to the future you want to create, and you end up once again struggling to "get things done."

Dr. Nadeau reminds us that two distinct parts of the brain are at work. "The primitive, reactive part of the brain deals with what comes at you. It's excited about getting things done. The higher, more thoughtful part of the brain is proactive—it's excited about getting the *right* things done. So, what's the consequence of trying to get through more and more of what comes at us? What happens when we overload the brain with too much input?

"As the brain gets overloaded, as you take on more than you can handle, as you deal with repeated interruptions and commands and conflicting demands, these deep, primitive centers of the brain get activated. You get distracted, you forget, you become inefficient, and you underperform."

The lower brain can get hooked on the lure of new texts just as a dog gets conditioned to salivate at the sound of a bell. Because we sometimes get useful information when we answer a call or read a text message ("Congratulations! You just won the lottery!"), we find ourselves mindlessly picking up and checking our phones every few minutes—whether anyone called or texted us or not.

So we're faced with an exasperating paradox. On one hand, we *feel* a surge of excitement when we even look at our smartphones. On the other hand, we *feel* overwhelmed when we see 1357 unread messages on the screen.

To make sure the higher brain stays in charge, you make Choice 4. You ensure that your technology works for you instead of against you. The Q2 Process Map below shows how to do that.

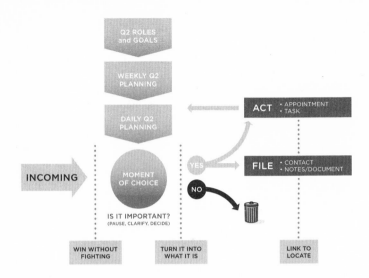

The Q2 Process Map. A flood of incoming information threatens to distract you from your Q2 Roles and Goals. Act on or file important information; delete the unimportant. Make the 3 Master Moves to direct that flow of incoming information so you can use it.

As a Q2 thinker, you use your finest efforts to advance your Q2 priorities. Any incoming message or request can disrupt those efforts. So you automatically pause and clarify: "Is this an important item? Will it help me advance my Q2 priorities?"

If the answer is yes, act on it or file it for future reference. If no, delete it.

Design a System to Manage the Core 4

If you're like most people, information comes at you all day from all directions. Your smartphone takes messages, texts, and tweets. Your email accounts fill up like a clogged sink. You take a phone call and write the message on any piece of paper that's handy. Your workspace is cluttered with letters, documents, and sticky notes. You might take notes on your phone or on your computer or in a notebook or on any available legal pad—or all of these. You tell yourself that someday, you're going to get it all organized, but it seems an overwhelming chore.

The Q2 Process can help you get control of this clutter.

The Core 4. Every incoming item of information can be classed as an appointment, a task, a contact, or a note. Act on appointments and tasks; file contacts and notes.

There are really only four kinds of information—appointments, tasks, contacts, and notes/documents. Think of them as the Core 4. The key to managing important information is to categorize everything under the Core 4.

As the Q2 Process Map shows, once you've decided an item is important, you have two choices: act on it or file it. If you can act on it, it's an appointment or a task and should go on your calendar or into your Master Task List for later scheduling. If you can't act on it, it's a contact or a note and should go into the appropriate file folder, either electronic or paper.

"EVERYTHING IN ONE PLACE."

Many people prefer to use a paper-based planner to track the Core 4. They have appointment pages, task lists, contact information, and notes pages all under one cover. The obvious advantage of this system is "everything in one place."

"EVERYTHING IN EVERY PLACE."

Other people track everything digitally. The advantage of this system is "everything in every place"—you can access the same information on your smartphone, tablet, or laptop if you have syncing capability.

Still other people have a blended system. You might prefer to record all your notes on paper—find a sturdy notebook and keep it within reach so anything you write goes there. If you use an information-management app like Lotus Notes or Microsoft Outlook, you can keep all your tasks in the task bar, your appointments in the calendar, and contact information in the contacts list. You might want to devise a system for cross-referencing your paper notes to digital information; for example, you could indicate in your calendar under a meeting appointment where to find notes you've taken to prepare for the meeting.

Whatever system you use, be consistent. It's easy to get into a real muddle if you have multiple calendars, to-do lists, and notes all over the place.

Make the 3 Master Moves

In the martial arts, a "master move" is a basic maneuver for defending yourself. To keep the onrush of electronic messaging under control, practice the following 3 Master Moves.

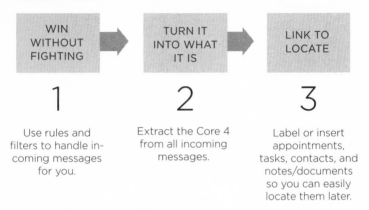

WIN WITHOUT FIGHTING	TURN IT INTO WHAT IT IS	LINK TO LOCATE
1	2	3
Use rules and filters to handle incoming messages for you.	Extract the Core 4 from all incoming messages.	Label or insert appointments, tasks, contacts, and notes/documents so you can easily locate them later.

Win Without Fighting. The story is told of a venerable karate master who tired of fighting young challengers. He easily bested them, but they never stopped taunting him; at length, he refused to take on any of them.

One day a particularly insistent challenger simply would not go away without a fight. So the old master said to him, "Very well, but I will not fight you here. We will fight on the island in the bay." So the two men got in a rowboat and made their way to the island.

When they arrived, the younger man jumped from the boat onto the shore ready to do battle. As for the older man, he simply rowed away, leaving his challenger alone on the island.

The moral of the story: The easiest battles to win are the ones you never have to fight.

Apply this lesson to your technology. Many of your emails are no doubt Q3—inconsequential, maybe even unsolicited. You can set up rules to route messages to the appropriate folders and to block unwanted emails.

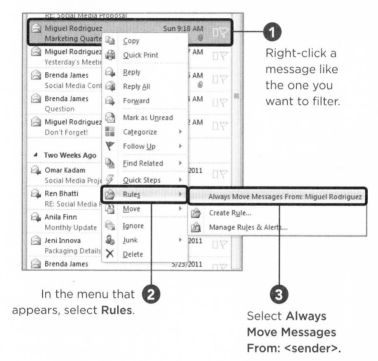

Right-click a message like the one you want to filter.

In the menu that appears, select **Rules**.

Select **Always Move Messages From: <sender>.**

4 In the Rules and Alerts dialog box that appears, navigate to and select the folder you want the messages moved to.

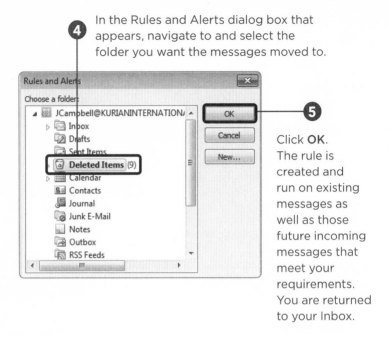

5 Click **OK**. The rule is created and run on existing messages as well as those future incoming messages that meet your requirements. You are returned to your Inbox.

Win Without Fighting. If you receive emails you don't want, follow a process like this one to automatically delete messages from those sources.

There's no need to spend your valuable time trying to figure out what to do with unimportant messages. If you don't create an automatic filtering system, you end up being the filter yourself, trying to wrestle with 500 messages a week. But you would probably rather be doing something important.

From the Q2 Process Map, you can see that this master move is your first defense against the "incoming." You'll never face a moment of choice over a message you never see.

Turn It Into What It Is. Go to your inbox. If you're like most people, you'll find there an intimidating, undifferentiated pile of gravel. As technology writer

David Weinberger says of the mass of electronic messaging we're subjected to, "Everything is miscellaneous."

If unimportant items somehow get through your filter, delete them.

Then turn important messages "into what they are." Categorize each item as one of the Core 4—as an appointment, a task, a contact, or a note. Tasks go on your task list, appointments into your calendar, and notes into appropriate subject folders. Of course, add contacts to your contacts list. Some personal-management apps let you drag and drop tasks into your task bar, appointments into your calendar, and so forth.

Turn an Email Into an Appointment. Click the email and drag it into your calendar. Assign it a time, save it, and close.

This master move is your second line of defense, as you sort incoming items into their proper categories. Schedule brief appointments with yourself—maybe two or three times a day—to "turn your messages into what they are" and make them actionable. Then you can stop worrying about what's sitting in your inbox. It will be empty.

Link to Locate. Some important messages connect with others. For example, you might receive an email from a customer related to an upcoming meeting. You can electronically link the email with the appointment so you don't have to look for it later.

In the figure below, you have an appointment with Ren to finish preparing a customer-feedback report. You can select the actual draft report and drop it right into the appointment; now you can access the report and the meeting information in one place.

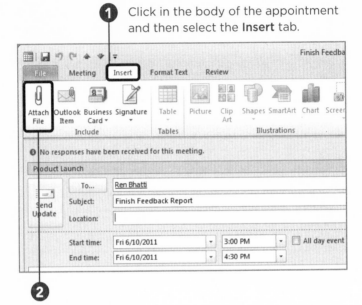

Click in the body of the appointment and then select the **Insert** tab.

Select **Attach File**.

In the Insert File dialog box, navigate to and select the document you want to insert.

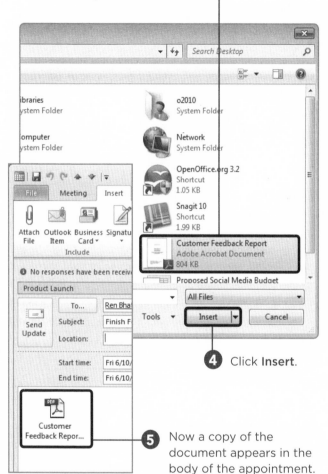

Click **Insert**.

Now a copy of the document appears in the body of the appointment.

Link to Locate. You can link a document to an appointment so everything you need for that meeting is accessible in one place.

In the day when information was recorded only on paper, things couldn't be filed in more than one place. But with digital information, you can put the same item in several relevant places. Suppose you are scheduled to give a presentation to your professional association. A lot of incoming information deals with that event. Or you receive an e-ticket for your flight, so you drag and drop it into the appointment on your calendar. But you can also save it in your airline-ticket folder. Someone sends you a report you can use for your presentation, so you drag and drop it into the appointment. But you can also save it in your presentation folder.

"Link to Locate" means you never lose track of important information because you can find it in multiple places.

The Q2 Process Map enables you to direct the flood of information into usable channels. You have now aligned your information tools so you can access everything you need quickly.

Use Productivity Accelerators

Now you can use your technology to accelerate your real work instead of hindering it—to get to what William Powers calls "the real magic of these tools, the catalyst that transforms them from utilitarian devices into instruments of creativity, depth, and transcendence." [26]

Your rule for acquiring technology is not to ask, "What's the latest and greatest?" but "Which tools will help me best achieve my Q2 Goals?"

Regardless of your objectives, there's usually "an app for that." There's no end to the wealth of applications for increasing your productivity—but there's also no end to the poverty of a life wasted on mindless technology.

Social media might be the most impactful tool for accelerating your productivity.

A community used to be a group of people in one location. Now a community can be a group of people who are never physically together but who share common goals and interests. This is the whole point of social media: Web-based and mobile technologies that enable people all over the globe to talk to each other at will.

Unfortunately, too many people use social media for Q4 purposes—as a seductive way to squander their time. The poster boy for Q4 is the famous character Richmond Avenal of the British comedy show *The IT Crowd*, who is so wrapped up in his technology that he forgets to eat and comes down with scurvy.

Think about how you as a person with a Q2 mindset might use social media: to do wide-ranging research, to test an idea on a lot of people at once, to connect with an old friend and renew a relationship, to blog about a key issue and invite ideas, to form a book club—the possibilities are endless.

Consciously live by these guidelines for using social media:

- Participate with a purpose: "What do I want to learn and why?"

- Follow the few: "Which few sites will help me achieve my goals?" Trim the time you spend on those that have nothing to do with your real priorities.

- Choose your level of participation: "Should I be a contributor, a joiner, or just an observer?"

- Create a "Q2 virtual community," a group of people who can advise you and whom you can account to in achieving one of your Q2 Goals.

- Subscribe to podcasts and blogs that help you with your Q2 priorities. One of the best things about social media is the flood of information and creative ideas you can tap into for your own purposes. For example, if you love news blogs, consider signing up for an aggregator service to simplify your access.

- Set up a time zone for reviewing the sites that are most important to you. Too many people fail to set boundaries on social media, and between Twitter, Facebook, email, and so forth, they end up trapped in Q4 before they realize it.

We invite you to check out The5Choices.com for evergreen thinking on how to increase your productivity. Here you'll find people sharing ideas on the best productivity tools, insights on getting the most out of your technology, and the views of the best thought leaders around the world.

Also, consult *The 5 Choices Technical Guide* companion to this book for ways to accelerate your productivity using the tools you already have.

Making Choice 4 helps you escape the technological trap that alarms neuroscientists such as Dr. David Rock: "I am sensing a dramatic upswing in people's sense of overwhelm.... It's social media. Like delicious desserts, it's hard to say no to. The brain loves it so (my brain included). Getting any work done these days with Twitter on in the background is like putting a ten-year-old child in a candy store and telling them they can't touch anything; they will be constantly distracted."[27]

Creating a system to master your technology isn't hard, although it takes a little investment of time up front. Once your system is in place, you'll find it easier and easier to say no to the "candy store" and to say yes to the Quadrant 2 life.

Teach to Learn

The best way to learn is to teach. Use the Q2 Process Map to teach others how to manage incoming information.

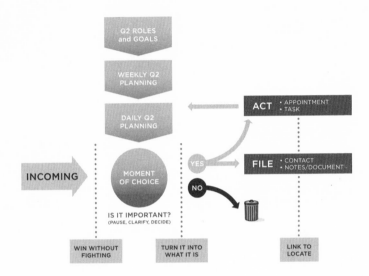

Choice 5: Fuel Your Fire, Don't Burn Out

"The energy of the mind is the essence of life."
— Aristotle

You've made Choices 1 through 4. A new sense of purpose governs your life, and you are excited about the extraordinary things you're going to do.

But if you don't have the physical and mental energy to follow through, you're likely to get discouraged and give up.

Our mode of life today—constant stress, poor diet, lack of exercise and sleep—leads to what scientists call "exhaustion syndrome." The rest of us call it burnout. We continually "push through" each day, postponing the renewal time our bodies and brains need. The mantra is "work like crazy and then crash." And we get rewarded for the ordinary mindset; it becomes a badge of honor to brag, "Our team was up till midnight." "I worked through the whole weekend." "Vacation? Are you crazy? No time!" But in the end, this pattern is killing our brain capacity, and it's no good for the organization either.

If we work in Quadrants 1 and 3 all day, strung out on urgencies and emergencies, we naturally end up in

Quadrant 4, numbing our minds with games or pointless Internet surfing or trash TV.

By contrast, extraordinarily productive people are wise enough to consistently recharge their mental and physical energy. Because they have a Quadrant 2 mentality, they maintain a constant flow of fuel to the mind and body so they can perform at their best every day.

There's a reason our hearts beat constantly instead of once a year: our cells need regular refueling. The greater the load on the muscles, the more energy required and the faster the heart beats to supply the glucose and oxygen that fuel the muscles.

There's a key principle at work here: You can't live on last month's meals, just as you can't draw strength from last year's purposes. You need to create a consistent rhythm of renewal, like the beating of the heart, to keep the brain and the body fully charged.

This is Choice 5: Fuel Your Fire, Don't Burn Out.

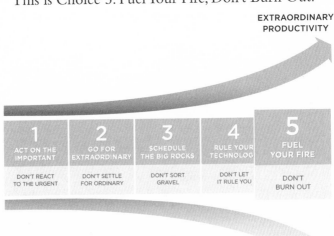

EXTRAORDINARY
PRODUCTIVITY

1	2	3	4	5
ACT ON THE IMPORTANT	GO FOR EXTRAORDINARY	SCHEDULE THE BIG ROCKS	RULE YOUR TECHNOLOG	FUEL YOUR FIRE
DON'T REACT TO THE URGENT	DON'T SETTLE FOR ORDINARY	DON'T SORT GRAVEL	DON'T LET IT RULE YOU	DON'T BURN OUT

BURIED ALIVE

You can't hope for extraordinary productivity in your work and life unless you make Choice 5.

Brain scientists tell us that mental energy comes from two sources: a high purpose in life and the right kind of fuel. If you've made Choices 1 through 4, you have a high purpose designed by yourself. Achieving what is meaningful to you requires expending energy, but it also fills you with energy. Professor David Ulrich says, "Meaning is not a dropped coin we pick up by chance. It is more like fine pottery we craft." If you love what you are crafting, you can put in unflagging work even when you're tired.

But a high purpose is not enough. Your brain also needs a constant, even flow of fuel.

Glucose is the fuel of the brain. Both lollipops and apples can provide glucose. But lollipops—or sugar drinks or doughnuts or candy bars—inject the brain with a huge hit of glucose that then drops off fast. It's like repeatedly racing an engine and wearing it out.

Because it metabolizes differently, an apple refuels the brain at an even, unbroken rate. It's like recharging a battery instead of blowing it up.

Extraordinary productivity requires the "apple approach." You can't race an engine at a high rate and expect it to perform well over time. Neither can you put your brain through the spike-and-crash cycle of modern life and expect to stay productive.

Now you say, "But I'm okay. I may be busy, and I may be under a lot of stress—who isn't?—but I'm not a burnout."

You can be pretty good at sporadic bursts of energy, but even at low levels, chronic unrelieved stress on the brain creates a kind of slow-motion crash. According to research by the Swedish psychologist Agneta Sandström, "Small daily stressors can accumulate to create chronic burnout."[28] It may be a long, slow decline, but it's a debilitating decline nevertheless.

Scientists agree that the drivers of brain health are exercise, diet, sleep, relaxation, and human connection. You can't expect to be extraordinarily productive unless the brain is clear, available to you, and running at optimum. What you do about one driver affects the others; and when you deliberately work on all five drivers, you generate a constant flow of energy throughout the day.

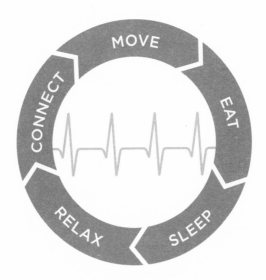

The 5 Energy Drivers. Brain scientists agree that proper exercise, diet, sleep, relaxation, and human connection recharge and even rejuvenate the brain.

Notice that none of the 5 Energy Drivers is urgent. As we've said, in today's workplace it's often a point of pride to neglect them; a busy person has no time for any of them. So we burn through the day on coffee—who has time for lunch? We put in long hours—who can get to bed at a decent hour, much less connect with family or friends? And exercise? "I don't have a minute to myself," we say, boasting about our intense busyness.

The 5 Energy Drivers reside in Quadrant 2; they are not urgent, but they are highly important. Twenty minutes of aerobic exercise in the morning creates new brain cells. A good breakfast and a lunch with friends are never urgent, but they power up the brain for productivity. During sleep, the brain grows novel connections essential to focused, creative work.

Choice 5 is not just about diet and exercise. It's about creating the conditions for optimum brain health and extraordinary productivity. People with a Q2 mentality work on the 5 Energy Drivers consciously and deliberately.

Move

Moving might be the best thing you can do for your brain. The simple act of walking measurably improves the brain's productive capacity. While sitting at a desk, you've probably experienced a "mental block" when you couldn't think; frustrated, you get up, walk to the water cooler, and suddenly everything becomes clear.

The human body was meant to move. Our distant ancestors walked everywhere, and we are physiologically programmed to walk 6 to 7 kilometers a day.

Students of the brain now know that aerobic exercise, which moves the large muscles of the body, stimulates the production of brain chemicals called neuromodulators, such as dopamine and serotonin. These chemicals govern mental focus.

When dopamine floods the prefrontal cortex—the executive center of your brain—your ability to focus and concentrate increases. When dopamine dries up, according to Dr. Manfred Spitzer of the University of Ulm, Germany, "the frontal lobes no longer do their job properly. [Speech and thought] are guided to a lesser degree...they become less planned and less goal- and thought-directed."[29] In other words, exercise tightens your mental focus as well as your muscles.

The more active you are, the more dopamine receptors in your brain; an obese, sedentary person actually has fewer dopamine receptors and, therefore, more trouble concentrating.[30]

Moving increases not only the brain's focus but also its capacity. Scientists once believed that the number of brain cells was fixed at birth, but we now know that's not so. "Nothing helps the growth of new brain cells more than aerobic exercise," says Dr. John Ratey of Harvard Medical School.

"Exercise itself doesn't make you smarter, but it puts the brain in optimal learning mode. Studies in rodents have showed that running leads to an increase in new brain cells in the hippocampus, which plays a large part in learning and memory. Also, studies of adults who exercise regularly show increased blood flow to the hippocampus."

Surprisingly, the benefits of one bout of exercise a day can be canceled out by sitting the rest of the day. "We're getting a new study every other week showing that even if you are in shape and you exercise, sitting kills your brain cells."[31]

Suppose you sleep 8 hours per day and exercise 30 minutes in the morning. The remaining 15½ hours are typically filled with home and work responsibilities that, more often than not, require prolonged sitting. You sit during the drive to work, at the computer before lunch, during lunch, in meetings after lunch, during the drive home, at dinner, and while watching TV at home. You might spend up to 95 percent of your waking hours sitting. The data indicate that this is typical for a majority of adults.

This lack of motion releases chemicals that put your body to sleep. They decrease blood flow to your brain, lower your alertness, and impair your thinking and judgment.

Fortunately, this problem is easy to solve. Get up and walk around!

If you sit at a desk all day, start your day with a 10- or 20-minute walk. Then take "brain breaks" periodically. Get up from your chair at least every 90 minutes to walk around, even if it's just to the coffee machine or to visit with a co-worker. Take a walk on your lunch hour.

"When you stand, your brain is acting 7 percent more effectively than when you sit because the large skeletal muscles are activated. Standing turns on the frontal cortex so you can think more clearly.

"The biggest challenge is to establish a routine and a ritual. We know how hard this is, but once you start, it takes on a life of its own. It's never too late. I know of 93-year-olds whose brains change when they start exercising. If you're in middle age and you start an exercise program, you'll push back your brain age 10 to 15 years."

It's a biological fact: An active body is essential for sustaining energy to the brain. What creative ways could you move during the day, given your work environment?

Dr. Ted Eytan of Washington, D.C., holds meetings on foot. He calls it "WWW—Working While Walking." "When you're scheduled to meet with someone, ask permission to try doing it on foot. If the answer is 'Sure!' meet the person at the appointed time and just start walking.

"It's a great way to bring fitness into the work environment. You can have a destination in mind, like the nearest coffee place, or not. You'll not only get business done, you'll enjoy a different kind of relationship building. There is something about sharing a walk with someone."[32]

Shimon Rura in Boston works a full day on a computer. Until recently, it meant he didn't get much exercise.

"Then I started using a treadmill desk. Rather than sitting, you walk at a slow pace. Because the human body has evolved to walk long distances, a healthy person can comfortably walk several kilometers a day. After just a few days, I was consistently walking six or seven hours.

"I love it. I'm not just doing something healthy without taking time from work. I'm working better because of the steady supply of exercise. My concentration is sharp and my energy level remains steady."[33]

Brain scientist Richard Restak walks at least three times a week "for a half hour to 45 minutes at a brisk pace in different locations around the city. That way I combine exercise with new surroundings, which keeps mental activity high."

"Consistent aerobic exercise leads to the growth of tiny new capillaries in the brain that bathe the neurons with nutrients. Anyone of any age who walks three times a week for 45 minutes will increase cerebral blood flow and improve their focus and attention span."[34]

Eat

Instead of recharging with healthy food, we often try to quick-fix our energy levels with refined sugars or artificial stimulants. This does indeed give us a spike of energy, but the boost is temporary; and this pattern damages our bodies and brains. It may get us through the day in the short term, but it's a poor substitute for the sustained, healthy energy we need for clear thinking and high performance.

"You can use food for better mental energy during the day, but you have to be smart about it," says Dr. Daniel Amen. "Start with high-quality calories. A 400-calorie sack of licorice is absolutely not the same thing as the equivalent in calories from a salad with a piece of wild salmon, blueberries, and walnuts." Dr. Amen gives these guidelines for fueling the brain:

- *Water.* Your brain is 80 percent water, and anything that dehydrates you actually steals your mental energy. It's important to drink six to eight glasses of water a day.

- *Protein.* High-quality protein is absolutely essential for the neurotransmitters that keep your mental energy stabilized.

- *Smart carbohydrates.* Take in low-glycemic carbohydrates that don't raise your blood sugar but are also high in fiber, which actually helps stabilize your blood sugar.

- *Healthy fats.* The brain is 60 percent fat. An intake of healthy fats helps you absorb nutrients and any supplemental vitamins you take.

- *The "Rainbow."* Eat foods with many different natural colors because they are filled with antioxidants that improve your energy and help keep your brain young.

"Most people eat lots of simple carbohydrates in the morning, such as pastries and cereals. It's a big mistake. Simple carbs drive down their blood sugar and they feel fuzzy and tired. It's much better to have protein in the morning—eggs, meats, nuts. Pancakes or pasta are much better in the evening when you don't have to focus."[35]

Additionally, the kinds of foods we eat may be less important to brain health than the number of calories we consume. Cutting calories slows down the onset of diseases like dementia, cancer, diabetes, and other illnesses associated with the loss of brain function. As a rough rule of thumb, a person who eats 35 percent fewer calories will live 35 percent longer, according to Dr. Restak.

"In order to tune up your brain and reduce your likelihood of Alzheimer's disease, you don't need to cut back drastically on your calories but simply keep your calories low enough to prevent obesity."

So how do you sustain an even glucose level during the day so you're not "spiking and crashing"?

Dr. Restak advises cutting back on the fast food that so many of us depend on at work. "Fast-food diets impair memory in some animals and make the brain more vulnerable to toxins. Reducing the amount of fat and empty calories in your diet might improve your memory and increase your resistance to diseases that stress the brain.

"Foods that slow the rate of cognitive decline include fruits and vegetables, especially green leafy ones that contain Vitamin E. Also, fish truly is a brain food. People with high levels of omega-3s from fish have lighter moods and much less depression. They also improve their memories. You don't have to eat a lot of fish—just a couple of servings a week seem to be enough."[36]

Sleep

When you're tired, the logical thing to do is to sleep. However, most of us are getting less sleep than ever—on average, 45 minutes less than just 25 years ago. Most adults are biologically wired to need seven to nine hours of sleep a night. When you get it, you're happier and more focused.

But when you don't, you build up a sleep debt and start to burn out. If you get less than four hours of sleep five nights in a row, you perform as if you were legally drunk. In today's high-stakes world, the last thing you want is impaired judgment, but that's what you get when you're not well rested.

In one experiment, participants who had just finished a training course were divided into two groups. One group was kept awake that night while the other group got a normal night's sleep. The next day both groups were tested on the skills they had supposedly learned during training. Those who had been allowed to sleep showed "a significant and continuous improvement of performance." The sleep-deprived group showed no improvement, and could not perform better, even after two more full nights of sleep.

A good night's sleep allows the brain to process what it has learned and to restructure itself around the new ideas. By contrast, "someone who continuously jumbles his natural day and night rhythm with artificial light, shift work, or keeping going all night impairs his memory."[37]

"In our hard-driving world, sleep gets no respect," says Dr. Restak. "The fact is, the more we sleep—up to a point, of course—the better we perform. Why is that? Well, think about tomatoes. During the day they store a lot of energy and at night use that energy for growth. A similar process occurs in the brain. During the day, the brain takes in a huge amount of information. At night, the brain, like a tomato, grows by changing its structure to accommodate the new information. The brain doesn't turn off during sleep. Because the brain is rebuilding itself rapidly based on the day's events, our dreams tend to be associated with what we learned during the day. The brain is literally building memories.

"Depriving your brain of sleep is like over-practicing a muscle. For example, if you practice a move in tennis, it will improve for a while. But if you continue beyond a certain point, you'll start to deteriorate as your muscles tire. So you stop practicing and let the muscles relax. The same is true of the brain. Sleep restores the learning circuits in the brain. If you learn something while awake, you can increase your chances of remembering it by 'sleeping on it.'"

So sleep makes you smarter. The brain restores and restructures itself around new information, generating new insights. How often have you struggled with a problem, gone to bed hopeless, and awakened with fresh answers? Dr. Restak recounts a famous experiment in which people were shown the letter sequence H I J K L M N O and asked to name one word this sequence reminded them of. No one came up with the correct answer, so the researchers sent them home to "sleep on it." Next morning, they reported their dreams. Several of them had dreamed of fishing or diving or sailing, which eventually suggested the right answer. The secret word was water — the sequence of letters was "H to O," in other words, H_2O, the chemical formula for water. Sleep changes our brains in a way that encourages the discovery of new and meaningful connections.[38]

Push yourself to stay awake, and you'll push yourself off the cliff of burnout and poor performance. It's just possible that your extraordinary life depends on getting a good night's sleep every night!

Relax

We live in a high-pressure environment. It's exhilarating, but it can also drain away our energy. While a certain amount of stress is actually energizing, if the stress goes on too long, it can turn toxic and damage our bodies and our brains.

Too much stress drains dopamine from the brain, reducing your power to think reflectively and assimilate new knowledge. Also, you lose your creativity. "Anxious people, generally speaking, only reproduce what they already know," according to Dr. Manfred Spitzer.[39]

You manage stress most effectively by making Choices 1 through 4, which puts you back in the driver's seat of your life. Additionally, new research shows the stress-relieving power of creating a rhythm of relaxation.

Dr. Agneta Sandström emphasizes regularly relaxing the brain. "It's okay to get stressed, but you also have to find time during the day to rest. Just as your muscles can get tired, so can your brain."[40]

It's essential to regularly disconnect the brain from the intense work of our busy days. When we create patterns of disconnecting, we create space for perspective and room to breathe, both physically and mentally. We make better decisions and increase our creative capacity.

When you disconnect, completely remove yourself from the pressures you are facing and any technologies that may interrupt you and engage in something totally different and totally enjoyable—whether alone or with others. If you find it really hard to disconnect from a stressful situation, that's generally a signal that you are stuck in a rut and need to disconnect more than ever.

The journalist Matt Richtel joined a group of scientists who experimented on themselves by totally disconnecting for several days. "They wanted to take a look at what was happening to their brain and their perspectives—and by extension, ours—as they got off the grid."

They took a raft trip down the San Juan River in southern Utah, one of the most remote places in North America. They had one unbreakable rule: no mobile phones and no Internet. "The reason why I say the rule was not breakable? There was no cell-phone coverage. There was no Internet. Right after we launched our rafts, one of the scientists said it's the end of civilization, by which he meant your cell phone will no longer work."

At the end of three days, the group noticed something happening to themselves. They called it "the three-day effect. You start to feel more relaxed. Maybe you sleep a little better.... Maybe you wait a little longer before answering a question. Maybe you don't feel in a rush to do anything. Your sense of urgency fades."

The scientists came away from the experiment with the "unequivocal" conclusion that downtime was essential for brain health.

This kind of Quadrant 2 downtime gives the brain a chance to process information and make sense of it. "Those neural networks and those new neurons make their way from the hippocampus, a part of the brain that's kind of a gateway for memory, into the rest of the brain. In short, during downtime, you record memory, you set the basis for learning."[41]

A vacation is extremely important for the brain, but you can give your mind a chance to recalibrate and rebalance in as little as 5 to 10 minutes during a busy day or in longer periods throughout the week. The idea is to build a rhythm of regular off time.

When stress is high, sometimes the natural tendency is to bear down and run faster. In times of extremely high pressure, however, it is more important than ever to stick to this pattern. Not only does it keep you healthy, but it improves your performance. Your thinking is more qualitative, your ideas more creative, your moods under control; and you simply perform better because you are keeping your fire burning instead of burning out.

Connect

Just as knowledge workers should *disconnect* periodically from their technology-driven days, they should *connect* with other people regularly and often.

In today's electronically interconnected world, it is easy to miss the one-on-one interaction that makes relationships strong. Taking time to reach out and engage with the important people in our lives can be incredibly rewarding and renewing. People who have a number of healthy, nurturing human relationships are far more re-silient and happy during times of challenge. If you keep to a rhythm of regular connection with these important people, you build a reservoir of energy. Plus, as you focus on contributing meaningfully to these relationships, your own worries fade and you gain a broader picture of life.

The brains of people who live constantly in the urgency mode are bathed in adrenaline and cortisol, the hormones that jolt you awake and keep you alert. "Stressed-out folks…can have elevated cortisol levels all day long. When your cortisol level is high, your body is stuck in fight-or-flight mode." Your veins and arteries are constricted, your blood pressure spikes; "chronically high cortisol levels can lead to a host of physical ills." You become negative, anxious, and unproductive.

The antidote to these stressor chemicals is another hormone called oxytocin, an "anxiety reducer," the "antistress chemical."[42] "Oxytocin," says neuropsychologist Sarina Rodrigues, is "a marvelous, amazing, and elegant hormone. It's related to generosity, trust, empathy.... It can actually calm the brain down. It can also lower heart-rate responses during psychosocial stress."[43] Professor Kerstin Uvnäs Moberg calls oxytocin "a ready-made healing nectar. Under its influence, we see the world and our fellow humans in a positive light; we grow, we heal."[44]

Oxytocin is released when we connect with people who are important to us. A touch, a warm handshake, or just being in the presence of a friend, a loved one, or a trusted co-worker can stimulate the production of oxytocin. It puts the brakes on stress. That's why regular and frequent connection with others is essential to your mental and physical health and, therefore, to your productivity.

Supposedly, we are more "connected" today than ever. We have Facebook friends, Twitter networks, and unlimited texting and mobile-phone minutes. As valuable as these connections can be, they do not take the place of actual human contact, of being authentically present to other people. Yet, technology threatens to supersede time spent with friends and family.

Dr. David Rock compares the digital kind of connection to empty calories. "I have a sense that we are rapidly moving toward giving people 24/7 easy access to 'empty neural calories.' These calories, in the form of perceived social connectivity, increase the overall stimulation of the brain, but may not do much to make our brains more integrated, adaptive, or functional. In fact, just like sugar, some types of neural stimulation leave you wanting more and more, without ever feeling satisfied. The result can be a reduction in healthy neural functioning."[45]

Real connection means showing affection, respect, and emotional support. It also means investing time. Lunch with colleagues, regular spouse or partner dates, one-on-one time with friends—these are Big Rocks in your schedule if you want to stay healthy and productive.

The 5 Energy Drivers are so crucial to your productivity that you should create Q2 Time Zones in your calendar for each of them.

To live your extraordinary life requires more than ordinary energy. Yet, so many of us are so worn out and worn down by the urgencies and emergencies of life that we end up suffering from a personal energy crisis. As with other crises, living in Q2 eliminates the energy crisis.

Making Choice 5 is not an ordeal but a release from useless stress, ill health, and loneliness. And it's easier than you think. A few minutes of exercise every day, sane eating habits, rest, relaxation, and getting together with people you like—these are not burdens but benefits. Establishing these few rituals can energize your life and make you exponentially more productive.

Teach to Learn

The best way to learn is to teach. Use the 5 Energy Drivers model to teach another person how to recharge mental and physical energy.

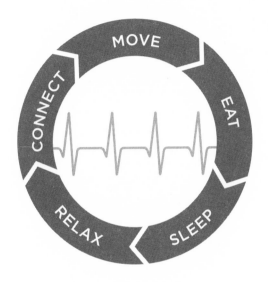

Your Extraordinary Life

"A man may be very industrious, and yet not spend his time well."
—*Henry David Thoreau*

You have now made the 5 Choices that lead to extraordinary productivity. You take the initiative to act on the "few and the true" most important priorities. You have a vision of the extraordinary things you can do in the essential roles of your life. You take charge of your time through thoughtful planning. Your technology serves your ends. You make time to nurture and energize your productive capacity.

To get the full picture of what these 5 Choices can mean to you, put yourself in the place of Jennifer in the stories below.

Life Before the 5 Choices

Jennifer arrives at work, opens her inbox with trepidation, and begins almost unconsciously to sort through and respond to the 50 emails that have arrived since she left the office the night before. Her Outlook rings to remind her of a meeting, to which she hurries off. The rest of the day, she bounces from the inbox to meetings with interruptions in between. She has no time for the critical thinking required to generate the exponential leaps her company needs to make. At the end of an overwhelmingly busy day, she is exhausted but left wondering what she's really accomplished. She's not sure how she can keep up the pace, but she's also afraid to slow down. She doesn't want to look like she's not contributing. At the conclusion of the workday, she collapses in front of the television and then repeats the pattern the next day.

Life After the 5 Choices

Weeks later, Jennifer excitedly comes into the office. Now she's confident. She knows where she's going in life and what contributions she wants to make to the company's future. Having already planned her week, she quickly checks her plan for those tasks that, if accomplished today, will have the highest impact on the organization and her personal life. During the previous weeks, she has successfully "detoxed" her inbox and has put in place rules and filters to win the email war without fighting. She also has new skills that make technology her servant and not her master. Because she has the habit of Weekly and Daily Q2 Planning, she's blocked out time for all of her important activities, including those that require critical, creative thinking and self-renewal. She knows when to say no or to negotiate a particular request. She knows how to effectively manage her capacity and energy for work and understands the science behind effective change. She has a mindset that enables her to self-orient toward the important and to make significant contributions at work and in life.

Whether or not your life is like Jennifer's "before" life, your future life can mirror Jennifer's after she made the 5 Choices. We've known thousands of people like Jennifer, and we've seen and rejoiced in the extraordinary lives they lead. We know it can happen for you too.

The 5 Choices are before you. May you choose wisely.

Notes

1. See "Time Matrix Survey" at The5Choices.com.

2. Nicholas Carr, *The Shallows: What the Internet Is Doing to our Brains*, 2010, pp. 5-16.

3. Mark Liberman, "Zettascale Linguistics," upenn. edu, http://itre.cis.upenn.edu/~myl/languagelog/archives/000087.html. Nov., 12, 2010.

4. Lynn Stanton, "Exaflood Could Be Zettaflood by 2015," Telecommunications Reports Daily, Oct. 1, 2007. http://www.discovery.org/a/4239. Nov. 12, 2010.

5. Jonathan B. Spira, "The Knowledge Worker's Day: Our Findings," Nov. 4, 2010. Basexblog.com, http://www.linkedin.com/news?viewArticle=&articleID=238699716&gid=1913261&type=news&item=238699716&articleURL=http%3A%2F%2Fwww%2Ebasexblog%2Ecom%2F2010%2F10%2F28%2Fwhat-we-learnt%2F&urlhash=WkV9.

6. "Email Statistics Report 2010-2014," The Radicati Group, http://www.radicati.com/?p=5290; Message Labs Intelligence 2010 Security Report, info@messagelabs.com, p. 6.

7. LexisNexis, "2010 International Workplace Productivity Survey: Too Much Information," http://www.lexisnexis.com/media/press-release.aspx?id=128751276114739.

8. Stephen R. Covey, *The 7 Habits of Highly Effective People*, New York: Simon & Schuster, 1989, p. 158.

9. Cited in John Naish, "Is Multitasking Bad for Your Brain?" Mail Online, Aug. 11, 2009. http://www.dailymail.co.uk/health/article-1205669/Is-multi-tasking-bad-brain-Experts-reveal-hidden-perils-juggling-jobs.html.

10. Cited in Carr, *The Shallows*, p. 140.

11. Interview with Dr. Ed Hallowell, Feb. 20, 2011.

12. See "Time Matrix Survey" at The5Choices.com.

13. Helke Bruch, Sumantra Ghoshal, "Beware the Busy Manager," *Harvard Business Review*, Feb. 2002.

14. William Powers, *Hamlet's BlackBerry*, New York: Harper-Collins, 2010, p. 27.

15. Powers, p. 27.

16. James Loehr, Jack Groppel, "Extraordinary Productivity," *Chief Learning Officer*, May 17, 2004, http://clomedia.com/articles/view/extraordinary_productivity

17. Elkhonon Goldberg, *The Executive Brain*, Oxford University Press, 2001, 2.

18. Interview with Dr. Richard Restak, June 18, 2011.

19. Covey, p. 156.

20. Interview with Dr. Daniel G. Amen, June 2, 2011.

21. Powers, p. 13.

22. Dr. Heidi Grant Halvorson, "The 3 Biggest Myths About Motivation That Won't Go Away," *Fast Company*, Jun. 1, 2011, http://www.fastcompany.com/1756747/the-3-biggest-myths-about-motivation-that-won-t-go-away.

23. Interview with Dr. Heidi Halvorson, June 28, 2011.

24. Jeff Brown, Mark Fenske, *The Winner's Brain*, Cambridge MA: Da Capo Press, 2010, pp. 38, 72.

25. Interview with Dr. Kathleen Nadeau, June 26, 2011.

26. Powers, p. 31.

27. David Rock, "Are Our Minds Going the Way of Our Waists?" *Huffington Post*, Jan. 5, 2009, http://www.huffingtonpost.com/david-rock/are-our-minds-going-the-w_b_389163.html.

28. Carrie Arnold, "Burnout Gains More Recognition Among Psychologists," *Scientific American*, May 9, 2011, http://www.scientificamerican.com/article.cfm?id=depressed-or-burned-out.

29. Manfred Spitzer, *The Mind Within the Net,* Cambridge, MA: MIT Press, 1999, pp. 277, 284.

30. "Scientists Find Link Between Dopamine and Obesity," Brookhaven National Laboratory news release, Feb. 1, 2001, http://www.bnl.gov/bnlweb/pubaf/pr/2001/bnlpr020101.htm.

31. Interview with Dr. John Ratey, July 12, 2011.

32. Ted Eytan, "The Art of the Walking Meeting," Ted Eytan, MD Blog, Jan. 10, 2008, http://www.tedeytan.com/2008/01/10/148.

33. Shimon Rura, "The Treadmill Desk: Exercise for the Sake of Hacking," Shimon Rura's Blog, Nov. 14, 2007, http://rura.org/blog/2007/11/14/the-treadmill-desk-exercise-for-the-sake-of-hacking/.

34. Richard Restak interview, Jun. 18, 2011.

35. Daniel Amen interview, June 20, 2011.

36. Richard Restak interview, Jun. 18, 2011.

37. Manfred Spitzer, "Learning During Sleep: Offline Reprocessing," Jul/Aug 2005, Education Ministerial Meeting, Organization for Economic Cooperation and De-

velopment, http://www.oecd.org/document/38/0,3746, en_21571361_44559030_35302118_1_1_1_1,00.html.

38. Richard Restak interview, Jun. 18, 2011.

39. Spitzer, *Inside the Net*, p. 275.

40. Arnold, "Burnout."

41. Matt Richtel, "Digital Overload: Your Brain on Gadgets," Fresh Air, National Public Radio, Aug. 24, 2010.

42. Susan Kuchinskas, *The Chemistry of Connection,* Oakland CA: New Harbinger Publications, 2009, pp. 8, 10, 52, 76.

43. Joe Palca, Flora Lichtman, *Annoying: The Science of What Bugs Us,* John Wiley & Sons, 2011.

44. Kerstin Uvnäs Moberg, *The Oxytocin Factor,* Da Capo Press, 2003, p. x.

45. David Rock, "Are Our Minds Going the Way of Our Waists?" *Huffington Post,* Jan. 5, 2009, http://www.huffingtonpost.com/david-rock/are-our-minds-going-the-w_b_389163.html.